Community
Quilts

Community Quilts

How to Organize, Design & Make a Group Quilt

KAROL KAVAYA
AND
VICKI SKEMP

LARK BOOKS
A Division of Sterling Publishing Co., Inc.
New York

KAROL'S DEDICATION
*To Vicky Owen, who introduced me to quilting. To Stephen Seal.
And to my husband, Tom. I couldn't have done it without you.*

VICKI'S DEDICATION
*To my great, great aunt Georgia Morris, who I never met but whose quilts taught me the joy of color and design. And to my grandmother,
Ruby Northcutt and several excellent aunts—Mildred Stubbs, Tellie Northcutt, and Marion Hinton—
who taught me to sew. And, of course, to Johnny, for all the years.*

AND TO THE QUILTERS,
*many of whom are quoted
throughout this book*

Sheila Adams
Susan Adams
Betty T. Anderson
Fay Atwater
Allegra Aylward
Laura Ball
Peggy Barnes
Peggy Banks
Linda Biggers
Patty Bradach
Mary Brumo
Jack Chaney
Roxann Colwell
Katie Cunningham
Nancy Darrell
Mary Eagle
Cheryl Ezell
David George
Kathryn Graeter
Andrea Graham
Doré Hansel
Ruth Hartzler
Rita Hayes
Nancy Hayes
Kathy Hendricks
Jo Hogan
Glenda Jones
Louise Killian
Jo Ann Klontz
Barbara Knight
Ginny Koranek
Cindi Kulp

Eileen Kulp
Margaret Lane
Louise Langsner
Betsy Love
Silvia McConnell
Jill Meier
Esther Moriarty
Lyn Owen
Vicky Owen
Jane Peebles
Laurie Peterson
Gitte Rehberg
Jane Renfroe
Candace Rice
Sara Sagar
Meg Saunders
Susan Sawyer
Doreen Shealy
Susan Sherard
Clare Smith
Shelia Spicola
Leslie Stilwell
Ida Thompson
Bobbie Tousey
Ruth Uffelman
Elisabeth Vierengel
Judy Welder
Libby Woodruff
Myra Zeller

Some of these folks only worked on a few quilts; others have worked on almost all of them. We apologize to anyone we have left off this list. We should have done this when we still had reliable memories.
—K.K. and V.S.

Editor: Jane LaFerla
Art Direction and Production: Celia Naranjo
Photography: Evan Bracken
Illustrations: Karol Kavaya
Production Assistance: Hannes Charen

Library of Congress Cataloging-in-Publication Data

Kavaya, Karol.
    Community quilts : how to organize, design, and make a group quilt/by Karol Kavaya and Vicki Skemp.
       p. cm.
    Includes bibliographical references and index.
    ISBN 1-57990-181-6 (hbk.) 1-57990-377-0 (pbk.)
    I. Patchwork. 2. Quilting. 3. Patchwork quilts. 4. Group work in art—United States. I. Skemp, vicki. II. Title

TT835.K383 2001
746.46—dc21   00-46378

10 9 8 7 6 5 4 3 2 1

Published by Lark Books, a division of
Sterling Publishing Co., Inc.
387 Park Avenue South, New York, N.Y. 10016

First Paperback Edition 2002
© 2001, Karol Kavaya and Vicki Skemp

Distributed in Canada by Sterling Publishing,
c/o Canadian Manda Group, One Atlantic Ave., Suite 105
Toronto, Ontario, Canada M6K 3E7

Distributed in the U.K. by:
Guild of Master Craftsman Publications Ltd.
Castle Place, 166 High Street, Lewes East Sussex, England BN7 1XU
Tel: (+ 44) 1273 477374, Fax: (+ 44) 1273 478606,
Email: pubs@thegmcgroup.com, Web: www.gmcpublications.com

Distributed in Australia by Capricorn Link (Australia) Pty Ltd., P.O. Box 704, Windsor, NSW 2756 Australia

If you have questions or comments about this book, please contact:
Lark Books
67 Broadway
Asheville, NC 28801
(828) 236-9730

Printed in China
All rights reserved
ISBN 1-57990-181-6 (hbk.) 1-57990-377-0 (pbk.)

Table of Contents

Introduction

AMONG THE MANY NEEDS felt by human beings are the desires to communicate, to form communities, and to create. In our busy world, it is often difficult to find, let alone build and nurture, community. And it is even harder to share in a group activity that feeds the creative spirit. From our own personal experience, we have found that group quilting meets these needs. Though you may think that group quilting is a quaint, country tradition from a bygone era, indeed, it is a vital activity that is practiced as much today in big cities and sprawling suburbs as it is in isolated rural areas. Women from all walks of life continue to experience the fullness of community through group quilting. In joining together to make a quilt for a chosen recipient, we extend an embrace that acknowledges the elements of life from joy to grief, welcome to farewell, noteworthy accomplishments to everyday milestones.

We've structured our book for you, the reader, into both an inspirational and practical manual to help you begin your own group quilt. The quilts in our gallery represent the history of our community, spanning a period of more than 20 years. During that time, we grew from strangers to friends. You could say we built our community stitch by stitch. To this day, the bonds we share create a fabric that is strong and true. In fact, the more we think about it, a community comes together like the pieces of a quilt—some pieces are bright, others subtle, but all of them bring out the best in each other when melded together into a harmonious whole.

Building Community

This book was inspired by women who found themselves part of a new life in which quiltmaking became a common activity. From

the first quilt we made together, we found that group quilting became an important part of our lives and a major factor in giving us that sense of community that seems to be missing in so much of modern life.

Over the quilting frame, women who may have just met learn more about each other. The physical nearness (sometimes hip to hip and knee to knee), the extended time (most quilting sessions last all day), even the shared meal (everyone brings something for a potluck lunch), all foster a feeling of closeness. Often one finds that confidences are being exchanged, feelings aired, and problems discussed in an extremely nonthreatening, informal group-therapy sort of a way.

Over the years, we've heard about problems with husbands, siblings, children, parents, co-workers, bosses, pets—all confidences imaginable—from the deeply disturbing to the pretty silly. Early on, pregnancy and child rearing were major topics, and we exchanged ideas and solutions as well as reassurances; "Really, eventually the baby will sleep through the night." Nowadays, aging, menopause, and car-

ing for elderly parents are common themes for our quilting frame symposiums; "Really, eventually the hot flashes will stop, and you'll sleep through the night."

The simple act of discussing problems often reveals that they are common to others and generally can be solved. Knowing others share these experiences is most helpful.

Sometimes, even those who aren't present that day at the quilting group can benefit—"So where is Mary Jo—I haven't seen her for ages?" And then someone tells the group that Mary Jo is having a bad time with whatever. And now the community knows that one of its members has a problem that may be eased with a friendly phone call, an offer to babysit, a job, a lawyer, a place to rent—the feeling of commitment to each other is reinforced.

The physical act of quilting, the simple mindless, repetitive act of driving the needle through the cloth, can be mentally soothing. One of our group, while in her mid-fifties, has fallen victim to an as yet undiagnosed mental ailment, a dementia of unknown origin. Yet once a week she quilts. A friend pieces a pillow top for her and helps her to begin each line of quilting along a strip of masking tape.

Though often anxious and afraid, she says that she feels at peace while quilting, and her home is warmed by the cheerful colors of some of her pillows—others, she has presented to friends and caregivers. Quilting continues to provide her with an outlet for creativity, a sense of self-worth in completing a project, and the opportunity to express her naturally giving personality.

How to Use this Book

This book will help you design, organize, and make a group quilt. The process is very simple. Since the quilt is to be given away, a recipient is chosen. The quilt is designed in block fashion, with individual blocks pieced together to make the quilt top. Participants receive kits for making their blocks, then send the finished blocks back to the organizer. The organizer pieces the top together, then gathers a group to do the quilting in a series of quilting bees. Finally, the quilt is presented to the recipient at a special surprise party.

Throughout the book look for quotes from the quilters. We hope their words will encourage and inspire you to make your own group quilt.

Starting Your Quilt

Whatever your situation or lifestyle, no matter where you live, you can make a group quilt. All you need are two or more people interested in quiltmaking, even if only one of them has a rudimentary knowledge of sewing. The second part of our book is a practical manual that will lead you step by step through the process. If you don't think you have the skill, we encourage you not to let this hold you back from this joyful, sharing endeavor. We did it, and so can you! Read through this book—and then do it!

Because many of us in those early years were stay-at-home wives or mothers, our schedules were flexible enough that we could find the time and opportunity to work on quilts. But quiltmaking, and especially group quiltmaking, can be for anyone, no matter how busy they are. One advantage of group quiltmaking is that one person doesn't carry the entire load. The desire to create and the willingness to work with others are all that is needed.

Many people would like to be a part of quiltmaking but are timid about leaping into it on their own. For these, an invitation to work on a quilt with others will give them their start. To find potential quilt mates, look to your activities and lifestyle: your office or work associates, your book club, P.T.A. parents, fellow church members, acquaintances from the gym,

your Girl Scout troop, fellow garden club members (you can't be outside all the time), or your own family members.

If your new group consists mainly of people who don't know each other very well, a fund-raising quilt may be a good choice for your first project. For instance, women from the P.T.A. might make a quilt to raffle to raise money for new library books, or church members could work to benefit their outreach program. Our group has made raffle quilts for the animal

shelter, the library, and a local peace group. On the other hand, if your group consists of close acquaintances, weddings, new babies, friendship, major birthdays, or anniversaries all give you plenty of opportunity to make a group quilt.

Whether you begin your quilt with a group of ready-made friends, or are gathering new acquaintances together, the process of making a group quilt will soon begin to work its magic. Before you know it, you'll feel a bond with your

I had... never done any quilting nor handiwork...

it was so interesting to me how everyone just assumed I would do a good job. I remember working on the butterfly quilt for Fay Skemp (Atwater) and, never having embroidered, I was terrified that I would mess up the whole project. We all got together at Libby's, and everyone was very helpful. It's hard to describe the feeling that I remember—it was like, "Don't worry about it, Ida. You'll do fine. We have faith in you." This from women who didn't know me well at all, and they weren't just saying it. They were sincere. I did get through that quilt and it (the embroidery) wasn't too awful. But I came away with such a sense of peace and acceptance that it made me look forward to future quilt projects and new skills. —I.T.

These group quilts were the way I met all my friends here and got to know them. There's nothing like sitting for hours around a quilt and just talking. —C.R.

The art, joy, and evolution of quilting is how I would best describe the experience I have had quilting with the women in Madison county…The art of quilting because the quilts are consciously planned and designed…The joy of quilting because it is a joyous experience to be able to create a product of love and beauty for another person, especially when that person is a friend…The evolution of quilting because many women went from novices to master designers and quilters…For me, the whole quilting process has been an enlightening experience, one from which I have collected significant remnants to nurture my artistic growth and enhance my relationships with others. —L.B.

quilt mates, and you'll find yourself part of a new and growing fellowship. It's hard to say who benefits most from group quilting, the recipient or the quilters. The recipient receives a true labor of love, a gift that warms the heart and one far superior to any you can purchase, while the quilters experience the deep joy found in sharing, creating, and giving.

TRADITIONS

Textiles and quilting have long been integral parts of many cultures. The color explosions of Amish quilts allow these "plain people" to express a love of color and design not otherwise apparent in their lives. African-American quilts have a certain wild exuberance provided by a wide variety of color and fabrics as well as a fine disregard for tedious detail. They are a good example of working with the material at hand, as are the Appalachian quilts made from feed sacks, tailors' samples, and end-cuts from garment factories. All show a joy in creation that extends far beyond the simple utilitarian goal of providing warm bedcovering.

Who We Are

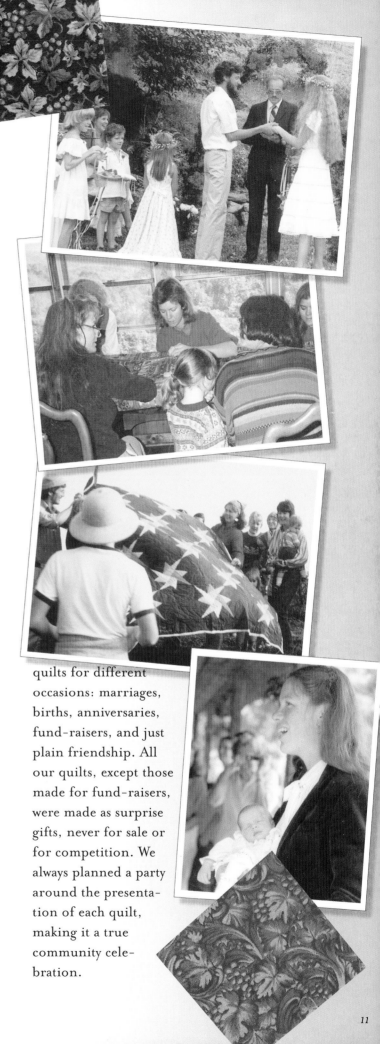

GROUP QUILTING BECAME A PART OF OUR LIVES IN A most natural way. In the mid-1970s we were among the first of the "new people" to move to our rural North Carolina county. For the most part, we were city or town dwellers who had come from all over the country, as well as from other parts of the state, drawn to what we thought would be a peaceful life in the country. We came from diverse backgrounds- teachers, artists, postal employees, the military, nurses, and quite a few of us fresh from school.

In 1979, the first wedding among the newcomers was announced. Some of us came up with the idea of making a quilt for the newlyweds, because we assumed "that's what you do" in the country. Four women had sewing and quilting skills, but most did not. For this first project, a few women did the bulk of the work, with many neighbors adding the quilting stitches.

Though quilting is a well-established tradition in our Appalachian area, most of us got our beginning information from books and from each other, rather than from our local neighbors. Our early quilting bees were learning experiences for most of the partic- ipants. Even today, more than 20 years later, there is often a beginner in need of one-on-one instruction.

Newcomers continued to discover our area, and babies started coming. In 1980 our sec- ond quilt, a baby's wall hanging, was made. Interest in quilting had grown, and 15 women took part in piecing and quilt- ing Anna's Animal Quilt. We began to plan and make quilts for different occasions: marriages, births, anniversaries, fund-raisers, and just plain friendship. All our quilts, except those made for fund-raisers, were made as surprise gifts, never for sale or for competition. We always planned a party around the presenta- tion of each quilt, making it a true community cele- bration.

Creating the System

Each quilt taught us something new, and we began to evolve a system for making group quilts. We developed methods for planning our time, organizing the work, creating kits, and scheduling the quilting. During a peak period, between 1981 and 1985, we created 21 quilts and wall hangings.

Though the circumstances of group members have changed over the years, the basic format we've developed for producing a group quilt remains tried and true. In those first years, most of the women stayed at home raising children and gardens; some were self-employed. As the years passed, children became teenagers and many of the women went back to school or got full-time jobs; some families moved away. We have come to realize that when more of the women were at home, it was easier to involve them in the piecing as well as the quilting.

But, and most especially when working with difficult patterns, we have found it is more efficient for three or four dedicated women to cut out and piece the quilt themselves, then get help from others for the quilting. We can even involve those who have moved away, sending kits

for making blocks long-distance. Though most of the original group from the early 1980s now have more demands on their time, they are still eager and willing to devote time to working on a group quilt.

Standing the Test of Time

The peace and privacy we found when we moved here were welcome, but with the remoteness came the feeling of isolation. Our group was spread out geographically, many of us living as much as a 45-minute drive from one another. Part of the initial motivation for quiltmaking came when we realized that the work brought us together in an enjoyable social activity in which creativity filled a common need.

Now, many of us have lifestyles that keep us around people much of the time, and isolation is a thing of the past. Our desire to continue working on group quilts comes from other needs within ourselves. We know that we will have a wonderful feeling of accomplishment, see friends, and "catch up" with each other as we work on a quilt. After all this time, we are still in awe of the astonishing emotion we feel when we give someone the gift of time, love, and beauty that is a quilt.

After 20 years of working together to produce almost 50 quilts, we found that this *is* "what we do" in the country! Now what about you? We believe the system we developed for making a group quilt will work anywhere, whether you and your friends live in a city a few blocks or subway stops apart, or in the suburbs a short driving distance across town. Our book simply shares the system we developed through years of experience. We hope our story and quilts will inspire you to organize your first group quilt, and that the first will be only one of many made in the company of friends.

Many of us came to Madison in the mid-1970s; some left, more came. We met as folks, non-locals, seeking community. We were young adults, often far from home and relations, in a place where everyone seemed related to each other. However different those relations were among our neighbors, our connections as friends shared the newness of our choices in lifestyles, shared the freshness of our endeavors, and shared the joy of laughter and parties and friends getting together. —P.B.

I moved here in the fall of 1972. We enjoyed visiting and talking with Masey Forkner and Thelma Wild, two local ladies who encouraged us. Masey quilted whenever she had the time. She always said, "You have to finish the milking and the cooking and the cleaning before you do the quilting. Otherwise the milking and the cooking and the cleaning won't get done." —L.W.

Meeting new people was important to most of us, I think, because we desired a sense of "newcomer community." That's not to say we weren't welcomed kindly and generously by our "local" neighbors. I think we provided a source of entertainment and amusement for them, most of whom had never seen anything quite like us. They opened their hearts and lives to us, taught us the things we certainly needed to know, and gently teased us. After Heather was born, I got to know more and more women who also had children. (Somehow women with children find other women with children, don't they?) We started a food co-op which brought more new people together. The number of parties and get-togethers was increasing. Slowly the old places that had been empty for so long were filling up with newcomers. —J.P.

My mother taught me

to quilt when I was very small.
Her mother taught her. I finished a quilt
that my grandmother never finished;
when she died, we found it.
We were married 11 years before our first
child was born; I would dream of a baby
quilt for my baby! We were living in Char-
lotte when our first (Carson) was born, but
[were] still in close contact with our community in Madison County. It was a great
surprise (to receive a quilt) because I
thought we had been forgotten. —C.K.

The "holler" we moved into had three
couples living in it, about our age, all "newcomers." It was because of these folks that
we managed to stay here; moving from a
college town required more adjustment than
I ever imagined, and the transition was difficult. These "holler" friends told us about
any upcoming parties; very soon we had met
50 "new" people—astonishing!
I first learned to quilt at Vicky
Owen's house…I pulled up my chair with
the others…too shy and embarrassed to
admit I didn't know how to quilt. I watched
and tried to imitate the others. They were
helpful when I asked but otherwise treated
me like I was a Normal Quilter. I know I
didn't do a good job that day, but I enjoyed
the company and conversation so much that
I looked forward to another quilting
opportunity. They gently gave me the
confidence to continue, and I was asked to
participate in the next group quilt. —K.K.

Our Gallery

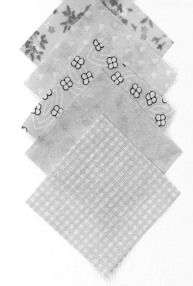

COME ALONG WITH US ON A 20-YEAR JOURNEY. See how our quilts evolved—there are creations to suit every taste and place. As you browse through the gallery, try to imagine how strangers to a region, and to one another, found something in the heritage of their new home that brought them together as a group.

Some of these quilts took hundreds of hours to complete, many of those hours spent in the convivial company of old and new friends. The subjects that we covered in conversation while quilting allowed us to get to know each other, and sometimes ourselves, better.

Every year we have a party in the spring. We gather the quilts together and hang them up for all to see. It is our time to remember, to reminisce, and to celebrate where we come from and who we are. These quilts are a record of our lives as a community. We hope that the quilts' stories will serve as inspiration for your own group project.

Each quilt has its own story and life.

I love to see them in the homes of my friends and in groups at the annual Easter party. I find myself longing to see a particular one sometimes when I have not seen it in a few years. —K.H.

The vast variety of quilts that we have made can only represent the vast variety of backgrounds, the medley of spirits, the patchwork of folks. Our quilts range from king-size crazy quilts to intricately designed wall hangings. We have covered the range of human experience: babies, friendships, graduations, weddings, anniversaries, good-byes, going-aways, and just because. —P.B.

We physically left the mountains in 1991 and are making our way in the "real world." Absence really does make the heart grow fonder. I spend some time each day missing the mountains and the people. In all my mental pictures and dialogues, the quilts are inextricably wound through the life we shared. —I.T.

1979

Maple Leaf Quilt

Size: 88 x 96" (2.2 x 2.4 m)

Designers & Organizers: Laura Ball, Betsy Love, Vicki Skemp, Libby Woodruff
Recipients: Paul Gurewitz and Silvia McConnell

THIS QUILT MARKS THE BEGINNING OF OUR STORY. This was the first time we came together as a group to make a quilt. As we were trying in our lives to get back to simple country ways, the idea of presenting a newly wed couple with a handmade quilt seemed fitting. Four of us got together to organize the surprise.

Since the wedding was to be in October, with the ceremony taking place under a big tree, the Maple Leaf pattern in fall colors seemed a perfect choice. The organizers assembled a list of all the couple's friends and sent them templates of the pattern with instructions for assembly. Participants were told to choose cotton fabric, using blue for the background and autumn colors for the leaves. Everyone was urged to make several blocks.

As the completed blocks trickled in, it was clear that there weren't enough. The four organizers met several times with their scrap bags and sewing machines to produce more blocks in an assembly-line fashion. With all 63 blocks at last in hand, the workers laid them out, trying various configurations to balance the colors. At last the huge top was ready for quilting. The women—liberated, nonsexist souls—decided that a quilting bee should include the men of the community. Enthusiastic quilters squeezed a gigantic frame into a tiny living room, and one of our typical potluck parties ensued.

The men, strange to say, were more interested in partying than quilting, and not a lot of serious work got done that night. Our group never repeated the experiment, but everyone finds delight in the various crooked stitches put in by hands more accustomed to hammers and chain saws.

Along the border of the quilt was embroidered a quotation from Dante: *"O voi che per la via d'Amor passate..."* (O ye who walk Love's path). This quote was chosen by the Italian-speaking bride for the wedding invitations. Also embroidered along the edges were the names of the bride and groom, the date of the wedding, and the names of all the quilters. Reading these names years later reminds all of us of friends no longer here and of that rowdy first quilting bee.

Looking at the quilt 20 years later,

I am struck by how good it is considering how little we knew. The random choices of fabric are exciting, the blue backgrounds provide continuity, and the visual impact is considerable.—V.S.

The entire collection of quilts will be a historical treasure of our lives and lifestyles, for they are quilts that tell stories.—L.B.

1980

Celestial Quilt

Size: 38 x 59" (.95 x 1.5 m)

Designer & Organizer: Libby Woodruff
Recipient: Benjamin Amberg, son of Laura Ball and Rob Amberg

AFTER FINISHING THE MAPLE LEAF QUILT, through trial and error, our little group felt they knew what they were doing. Since one of the four organizers of that first endeavor was expecting, it was time to make a baby quilt! The designer decided on a celestial theme, then chose the background, border, and sashing fabric. She sent out the blue background pieces with sketches of the images she wanted each participant to reproduce. Needleworkers were free to use embroidery, appliqué, or both. For many, this was their first venture into either medium.

1980

Anna's Animals

Size: 38 x 50" (.95 x 1.3 m)

Designer & Organizer: Vicki Skemp
Recipient: Anna Woodruff, daughter of Jim and Libby Woodruff

THE PREGNANCY CONTAGION SPREAD—now another of our quilting group was expecting, and it was her turn to be surprised. For Anna's quilt, workers were given rectangles of green fabric and told to choose a familiar animal to embroider and/or appliqué. The tiny blue squares at the intersections of the sashing have insects embroidered on them. One inexperienced needleworker was having trouble representing horse's feet, so she put a flowery strip of fabric at the bottom of the square to depict the meadow in which the horse was standing ankle-deep!

The first quilt

we received was a baby quilt for our youngest daughter Anna, born at home early in the morning on September 27, 1980. I didn't know that a surprise party had already been planned for that day. The ladies who planned it didn't know that it would be the day of Anna's birth. So, grinning with joy and excitement, I proudly showed Anna to my friends. Grinning with joy and excitement, they proudly showed me the quilt that they had made for Anna! —L.W.

When we met for the party to present the quilt to the mother-to-be, we learned that the baby had been born that morning at home. So we tramped up the road from the original site of the party to the Woodruff house to meet baby Anna. I'll never forget Libby's tired, happy face as she looked at us in surprise and said to her mother, "These are...these are my friends." —V.S.

Lily's Baby Blocks

1981

What I remember most about receiving Lily's quilt was how incredibly beautiful it was, and the love that was sewn into it. This was a very emotional time—our first child and all these people had taken the time to create this gift for her. We knew the child was being born into the perfect place and time. The quilts are a tangible reassurance that that community really existed and still does. —I.T.

Size: 45 x 57" (1.1 x 1.4 m)

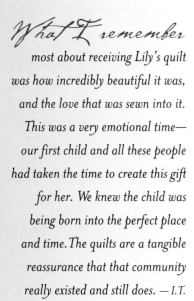

Designer & Organizer: Laura Ball
Recipient: Lily Twining, daughter of Roland Twining and Ida Thompson

LILY'S QUILT IS THE TRADITIONAL BABY BLOCK PATTERN with the addition of embroidery and appliqué within the blocks. The organizer chose the soft colors and tiny print fabrics. Like many of our group's quilts, it needs to be seen closely in order to appreciate the love and skill that went into its making. Laura's block, featuring the Raggedy Ann doll and ball, is the obvious work of a skilled and practicing fiber artist. But Jill's block, with the duck, the bunny, and the pig, is the amazingly well-executed labor of a first-time embroiderer.

1981

Circus Quilt

Size: 29 x 38" (.7 x .95 m)

Designer: Vicki Skemp Organizer: Glenda Jones
Recipient: Zeke Loomis, son of Chuck Loomis and Peggy Barnes

THIS IS A DEPARTURE FROM THE PREVIOUS BABY QUILTS which featured squares within sashing. The circus quilt was designed with various sizes of rectangles and with some images reaching out of their rectangles. The designer controlled the finished appearance of the work by giving participants exact patterns and materials. Several of the figures, the ringmaster for one, are stuffed and then appliquéd for a 3-D effect. The vibrancy of the primary colors is engaging to adults as well as babies.

The designs,
the colors, the fabrics, the handi-
work...a flower, a basket, a
fantasy creature, a butterfly, a
Noah's Ark animal, a circus ani-
mal. Each person's contribution
has been unique and specific for
that quilt, that gift. The stitches,
some fine, some random, some
erratic, all the threads that bind
us, that touch us, that connect
our community. —P.B.

1981

Jesse's Farm Quilt

I learned to quilt when we did Jesse Graeter's quilt. I was to appliqué the pig. Bob's mom did a lot of it, and I learned to appliqué then and quilt. That was the first time I really did meet Judy and Libby and Vicki. —S.A.

The idea of making a farm scene occurred to me because we all lived on our own "homesteads." It is put together like a puzzle. An overall drawing was made of the entire quilt. (The only requirement for a puzzle quilt is that it be put together in strips or parallel sections that are horizontal, while the vertical breaks do not have to match up to each other from section to section.) The quilt won a second prize in a local contest. —L.W.

35 x 52" (.8 x 1.3 m)

Designer & Organizer: Libby Woodruff
Recipient: Jesse Graeter, son of John and Kathryn Graeter

WE CALL THIS A "JIGSAW-PUZZLE" QUILT. The designer began by creating an overall picture—most of it drawn on freezer paper. Next, she divided the images into different areas and assigned each worker a scene or an object to appliqué and/or embroider. When the individual pictures were completed, the designer reassembled them. A quilt like this requires careful planning and a reasonably accomplished seamstress to piece it together.

1981

Butterfly Quilt

Size: 36 x 50" (.9 x 1.3 m)

Designer & Organizer: Vicki Skemp
Recipient: Fay Skemp Atwater

THE BUTTERFLY QUILT WAS DESIGNED TO REPRESENT CHANGE AND
PROGRESS toward the unknown. The recipient was moving to California
to work with Elisabeth Kübler-Ross, advocate for the dying, who is cred-
ited with starting the Hospice movement. The butterfly is a special symbol
in Kübler-Ross's work, an image from nature representing death and the
transition into the afterlife. Some of the butterflies on the quilt are
exquisite pieces of appliqué, reverse appliqué, and embroidery.

My first was Fay's butterfly quilt…I tried to stuff my
butterfly wings with feathers! Stupid—they
stuck out all over, and then I tried to burn
them off—of course this was the night before
the due date. The quilt was beautiful
regardless. —C.R.

Vicki Skemp invited many of my longtime
women friends over to say goodbye. Early
that day, I walked up the mountain to her
(Vicki's) house and said, "I'm not
leaving!" She said, "Okay, but we can still
have the party." I left satisfied, thinking
every issue had been resolved, and headed
down the mountain. Halfway down, I
turned back and reappeared in her (Vicki's)
kitchen. "Vicki, I'm going to California."
"Okay," she said. Much of the gathering
was a blur to me. Then I was presented
with a big box. Inside was the most beautiful quilt I had ever seen. At the moment all
I could see was the love of my friends who
had reached out to support me in my journey. The quilt was the only thing I took to
California besides my clothing. Eventually
my quilt and I found our way back home to
the family and friends who had so lovingly
stitched their way into my heart. —F.A.

1982

Noah's Ark

It was fun having my baby shower a week after the birth of my daughter Amelia. Everyone got a chance to hold and snuggle with her while I opened the mountain of gifts. Later, after refreshments had been served, I was summoned to the porch. There, hanging on the wall behind the swing was a beautiful baby quilt. What is so special is that there are so many different levels of talent represented. We all spent a long time poring over the squares, noticing each detail. —F.A

Size: 47 x 56" (1.2 x 1.4 m)

Designer & Organizer: Vicki Skemp
Recipient: Amelia Uffelman, daughter of Wayne Uffelman and Fay Skemp Atwater

FAY, WHO RECEIVED THE BUTTERFLY QUILT, eventually came back from California, got married, and later had Amelia, for whom this wall hanging was made. The idea for the design came from the picture of a hooked rug seen in a magazine. More than any other quilt, this one shows the range of skills in our group at this time. There is some fairly clumsy first-time appliqué and some incredibly beautiful embroidery.

1982

Dr. Heather's Good-bye Quilt

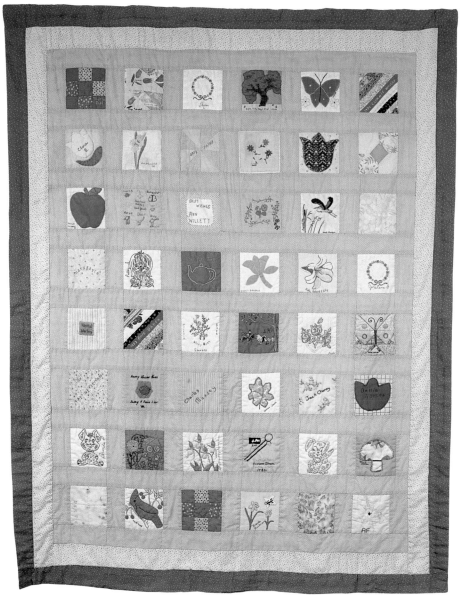

Size: 64 x 80" (1.5 x 1.9 m)

Dr. Heather
and my daughter Heather had a
special bond because they shared
the same name. Since the
squares on the quilt were "free
form" I decided that I would get
my Heather to draw some fig-
ures (they were just stick figures
because Heather was very
young), and then I embroidered
the figures.—J.P.

I rarely see Heather's quilt but I
remember the extra effort I put
forth to produce something of
beauty for her. All of the blocks
are very personal expressions of
love. Our hearts ached to see
her go! —K.K.

Designer & Organizer: Libby Woodruff
Recipient: Heather Spencer

DR. HEATHER SPENCER SERVED OUR COMMUNITY for several years
before moving to a larger practice. This charming quilter's choice quilt,
made as a going-away gift, contains blocks made by a broad spectrum of
people, many of whom did not know each other and many of whom did
not work on our other quilts. Their common bond was the beloved
doctor who had touched their lives.

1982

Octagonal Crazy Quilt

Designers & Organizers: Candace Rice and Rita Hayes
Recipients: Tom Donahey and Karol Kavaya

Size: 90 x 92" (2.2 x 2.3 m)

THIS QUILT WAS PLANNED QUICKLY for a couple who surprised the community with their marriage and the announcement that a celebration would follow in a few months. This was a time constraint that put some pressure on the group. Fortunately, one of the designers knew the bride's personal tastes and chose her favorite pattern, the Crazy Quilt.

Two women came up with a design that uses the crazy-quilt technique in a most unusual way. Each participant was asked to make a certain size block. These were connected by geometrical pieces of velour surrounding a central showpiece of white satin. The odd-shaped pieces and parts of this quilt make it a marvel of engineering. The satin portions of the quilt are filled with lovely feather-motif stitching. Velour is difficult to quilt, so this portion of the quilt is tied. (This is a good option and choice if you are limited in time.)

One appeal of the Crazy Quilt is that vintage fabrics look right at home in this pattern. In this quilt, one piece of lace came from the wedding dress of a quilter's grandmother. We believe details like that make the gift even more special to the recipient.

The first quilt

I organized was with Rita for Tom and Karol. How could I forget! We sat up quilting all night at John Henderson's the night before the wedding party. A crazy quilt—satin and velvet—with fancy feather quilting. My favorite of all I've done. I embroidered their names in the center and surprised myself at how nice it came out. —C.R.

Karol remembers: Tom and I got married in a quiet fashion with three witnesses and without telling anyone else. Two months later we had a big party in our yard to celebrate our marriage. Of course it was choreographed for me to open a certain present last.

As I opened it, even though it was the size of a folded quilt, that thought never crossed my mind.

It was impossible that a quilt could have been made for us in that short time! When I saw what the package held, I was shocked. A full-size quilt of such beauty and exactly my favorite—a crazy quilt—it took my breath away. I will never underestimate my friends again. —K.K.

1982

Dresden Plate Quilt

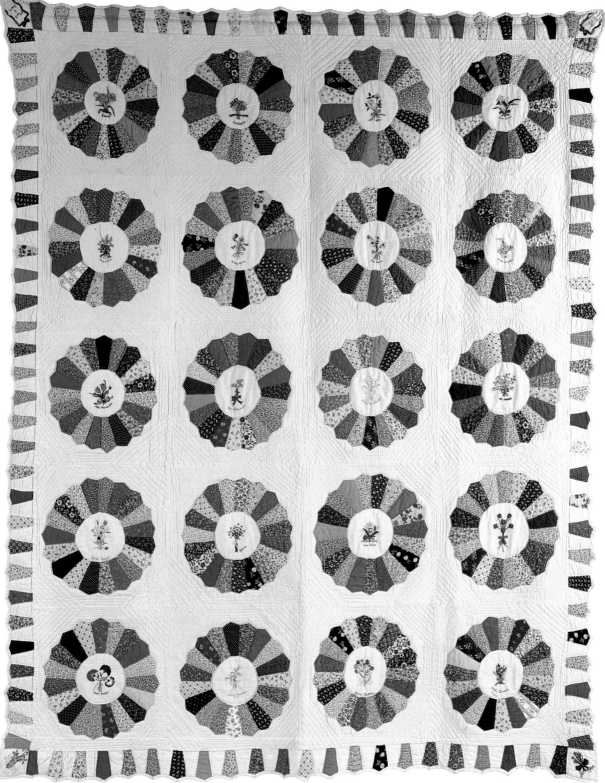

Size: 72 x 90" (1.8 x 2.2 m)

Designer & Organizer: Vicki Skemp
Recipients: Mark Anderson and Sara Sagar

THE WEDDING, THE OCCASION FOR MAKING THIS QUILT, was held at the summer home of the bride's parents in another town. Several weeks later at a party in our county, the group celebrated the event and presented the quilt. It is a very traditional pattern in old-timey calico prints that have been appliquéd on unbleached muslin. The participants personalized it with the untraditional addition of an embroidered bouquet in the center of each "plate."

When the quilt was opened up that hot, humid July day, I was overwhelmed by all the meticulously embroidered wildflowers, and thought about all those hands making all those stitches. —S.S.

A caring circle, an evanescent metaphysical joining together, creating a gift of loving kindness. —A.A.

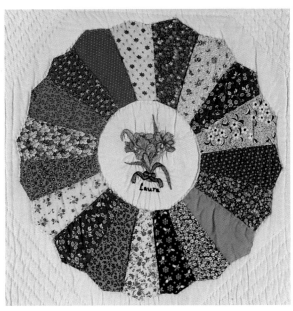

1983

Twentieth Anniversary Quilt

Size: 66 x 80" (1.6 x 1.9 m)

Designers & Organizers: Fay Skemp Atwater, Vicky Owen, and Susan Sawyer
Recipients: John and Vicki Skemp

THIS QUILT WAS PLANNED by the recipients' sister/sister-in-law, and another long-time friend, with design help from a visiting quilter. The pattern is, appropriately, Sister's Choice. The quilt starred at a surprise presentation party where the champagne flowed and all the ladies, without prior planning, wore shades of purple to match the gift!

Someone had to do it...

Vicki Skemp was often the guiding force behind many of the beautiful quilts created over the years. Everyone wanted to create one for her, but how do the uninitiated begin? Vicky Owen and I decided that, of course, we would easily be able to pull this off. Cutting out the pieces and making templates wasn't as easy as I had imagined. We checked and rechecked. We spent the day laying out the squares. This had possibilities... by nightfall we had the top pieced together.

I thought it was beautiful.

Later that night I received a call from Vicky, "I don't think this looks quite right." The next day she called several more times. A day later Vicky called yet again and said not to worry anymore, everything was fine. She went on to say she had taken our beautiful quilt top to Libby Woodruff. (Libby is a fine seamstress, always creating beautiful things.) I was getting excited. Did she like our top?...Vicky continued on, "Libby said it will be just fine; all she has to do is take everything apart and sew it together again."

For the party, everyone brought a bottle of champagne and lots of wonderful food. There were many stories about the mishaps, the panic, the fun. That's the magic. Each quilt has its own story to tell, marking a moment in time where friends came together in the unity of thought, word, and deed. —F.A.

When we brought the quilt home that chilly November night, we hung it on the wall opposite our bed. It seemed to glow with an inner light, and I kept waking up to look at it. What an amazing surprise! —V.S.

1983

Baskets With Flowers

Size: 67 x 84" (1.6 x 2 m)

Designers & Organizers: Libby Woodruff, Karol Kavaya, and Candace Aldridge Rice
Recipients: Malcolm and Vicky Owen

THE DESIGN FOR THIS QUILT came about because the organizers thought the recipients would like something traditional and because one of them had a well-known love of flowers. Three women spent an afternoon cutting the patterns of the various baskets out of freezer paper. The organizers asked each quilter to choose her own fabric for the basket. Putting together the little baskets with their tiny triangular pieces was unexpectedly difficult. But everyone put forth the effort and it was worth it—we think the final effect is charming.

When I received my quilt I felt elated and a part of our neighborhood and the county. —V.O.

This is one of my very favorites of all our work. I love the old-timey patterns, and the colors produce a lovely soft effect. —K.K.

One of the hardest things we have to deal with when making a quilt is keeping it secret. While we were finishing Vicki and Johnny's quilt, we were starting Vicky and Malcolm's quilt. It was so confusing to remember what to say or not say to Vicky and Vicki as we talked to or about them. —L.W.

I helped organize Vicky Owen's friendship quilt at Libby's. We did the baskets with embroidered flowers too. I did violets— Vicky's favorite. —C.R.

Birds

Astounding.

Everyone did a favorite bird. The embroidery and quilting are unbelievable. We won a group-quilt ribbon at the Cranston Quilt Show. Was so proud. Still am. —C.R.

Size: 70 x 86" (1.7 x 2.1 m)

Designer & Organizer: Karol Kavaya
Recipients: Candace and Steve Rice

THE DESIGNER WANTED TO CREATE A QUILT WITH A BIRD MOTIF, so when the opportunity arose to make a quilt for a nature lover, she was delighted. She asked each needleworker to execute a realistic bird using embroidery. Since the quilting itself was also very important to the designer, bird blocks were alternated with plain blocks on which heart and scroll patterns were quilted. The designer was also able to incorporate herons into the quilted border.

We receive many comments about an unusual feature of this quilt, the multicolored, diagonally pieced inner border. We believe it adds visual interest, color definition, and a certain sophistication. Wives, take note: this quilt is often a favorite with men.

1983

Adam Johnson's Quilt

THE DESIGNER CONSTRUCTED this striking wall hanging for a baby boy using strong colors and geometric shapes with lots of room for intricate quilting. The designer did all the piecing herself, then passed the quilt around to be quilted.

Size: 40 x 58" (1 x 1.4 m)

Designer & Organizer: Candace Aldridge Rice
Recipient: Adam Johnson, son of Rita Hayes and Jeff Johnson

Tilson's Fantasy Quilt

Size: 38 x 51" (.95 x 1.2 m)

Designer & Organizer: Rita Hayes
Recipient: Tilson Rice, son of Steve and Candace Rice

HERE'S A GOOD EXAMPLE OF A DESIGN for a baby quilt that came solely from someone's imagination. Again, as with the Octagonal Crazy Quilt on page 28, the designer planned the quilt with interesting geometric shapes. The navy blue pieces were cut out and sent to participants with the request that they put a favorite fantasy figure on them.

The designer made sure to give experienced needleworkers the corner and center pieces since those images were to be much larger than the rest. The choice of a dark background color adds drama and mystery. This quilt has lots of color, creativity, and whimsy—perfect for a baby!

We only knew local people at first. All were so good to us, adopted us, and gave us homegrown meat, milk, eggs, etc. After moving to Big Pine in 1978, I met Karol and the newcomers. Then came the quilts—a beautiful, magical baby quilt with fantasy figures and a unicorn in the center. It was perfect for Tilson. And Karol knew because she and Tom delivered him! —C.R.

Rita says that the theme for this quilt came from being the mother of a newborn herself. Seeing the world through his eyes made her feel as if the possibility of magic was everywhere… "magic was afoot!"

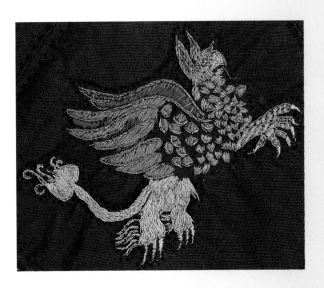

1984

Noah's Pinwheels

A Traditional pattern linking us to hands and minds and hearts of the past. —A.A.

For Noah ~ March 15, 1984

Size: 40 x 49" (1 x 1.2 m)

Designer & Organizer: Karol Kavaya
Recipient: Noah Twining, son of Roland Twining and Ida Thompson

THIS IS AN EASY, traditional pattern that any group can make. The organizer gave participants templates and instructions to use blues, greens, or pinks—one solid, one print. There is a narrow border and quilting that is a quarter inch from the seam. This quilt has a simple charm and is easy to accomplish for all skill levels.

1984

Rosie's Shoofly Quilt

July 6, 1984

Rose Mary
Anderson

Size: 54 x 54" (1.4 x 1.4 m)

Designer & Organizer: Vicki Skemp
Recipient: Rose Mary Anderson, daughter of Mark Anderson and Sara Sagar

THE SHOOFLY PATTERN, like the Pinwheel, is very traditional and very easy. Participants received templates for the square and the triangle. They were told to use fabrics in basic crayon colors (red, yellow, blue, green, orange, and purple), choosing a print for the background and a solid color for the geometric figure. Dark blue is always a good choice for unifying various colors, so it was used for the sashing and the border.

The quilting pattern included roses in the border in honor of the baby named Rose Mary. In 1998 the "baby," Rosie, then a 15-year old, made a lovely Star quilt with help from the designer of her baby quilt. It's fun to see a tradition renewing itself.

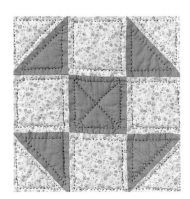

Peace Quilt

Each appliquéd square was designed by its maker to show something about her life that she wished to share. The idea was to let our images express the compassion and friendship that we felt. Working on the peace quilt was a powerful experience for me, both because of the great effort our community gave to the project and because of the power of the quilt itself. I felt it really carried our message clearly and would go straight to the hearts of those who received it. — L.L.

Designers & Organizers: Vicki Skemp and Louise Langsner
Recipients: People of Russia

OUR COMMUNITY ONCE HAD A SISTER CITY IN RUSSIA. One of our group had the idea to make a quilt as a special and appropriate gift for our new "friends." Lots of women, many of whom had not worked on any of our other quilts, wanted to be part of this project.

The designer chose the Attic Window pattern. Needleworkers were given their background square (the window), and asked to create an image that would tell something about their lives. Each was meant to help people in the Soviet Union visualize parts of a United States citizen's life and environment. Among the pictures on this quilt were a weaver, houses, flowers, children, a rainbow, animals, and, of course, a quilter.

Soon after the quilt was finished, a delegation of Soviet women visited a city near us. Included in the group was the wife of the well-known Russian journalist Vladimir Posner. Representatives of our group, knowing that Mrs. Posner spoke all over the Soviet Union and that she'd share the message of our quilt with many others, gave it into her keeping.

Making a quilt to "speak" to people in another country was a unique, rewarding, and enjoyable experience. We like to imagine that the pictures the Russian people see when they look at this quilt remind them of their own lives and highlight the similarities between us rather than the differences.

1985

Luke's Sister's Choice Baby Quilt

Size: 51 x 64" (2.3 x 1.5 m)

Designer & Organizer: Karol Kavaya
Recipient: Luke Rice, son of Steve and Candace Rice

YOU CAN ACHIEVE LOOKS that are vastly different from each other using this one traditional quilt pattern. As comparison, look at the 20th Anniversary Quilt on page 32. It is the same pattern, but there the designer chose fabrics in solid blues and purples. The rhythm of the repeated blocks and cool harmonies of the restrained color choices give it a contemporary, sophisticated air.

For Luke's quilt, on the other hand, more muted colors in a combination of solids and prints were used. Some prints were purposely chosen for their "old-timey" look. The contrasting colors of turquoise and red in the latticework and border enliven the quilt, making it more appealing for a baby. The designer's seemingly random placement of the blocks was actually carefully thought out. She felt that this contributed to the folksy feeling of the quilt, something she thought the new mother would like.

1985

Karol's Food Quilt

Size: 44" in diameter (1.1 m)

Designer & Organizer: Libby Woodruff
Recipient: Karol Kavaya

FOOD WAS THE OBVIOUS CHOICE OF THEME for this wall hanging made as a thank-you for the woman in our community who managed our food co-op for many years. Its unusual shape reflects the co-op's name, The Circle. The designer called all participants and asked them to choose which food item they would like to depict. She then drew the design on the fabric and passed it around for embroidery or appliqué. This piece displays some beautifully executed work.

Round quilts are not easy to hang. Our solution to the problem is to sew a semicircle of fabric on the back of the quilt, then cut a piece of corrugated cardboard to fit in the pocket. This stabilizes the top half of the quilt so that its sides hang correctly.

Karol's perseverance and dedication to keeping our food co-op running for so many years earned her this quilt. I felt it would be a good idea to draw fruits and vegetables on the fabric and pass it from house to house so that each person could appliqué or embroider directly on the circle of fabric. —L.W.

(At the Presentation Party)
I don't remember any words that were said, but I remember all of us being asked to gather. I remember Peggy Banks and Vicky Jorgensen smiling at me, and Anna Woodruff came over to me while her mother Libby started to give a speech. Everything had gone into slow motion because I realized I was being honored. The words of praise and thanks were enough to touch me deeply; when they handed me my wall hanging, I went into another state of consciousness! —K.K.

ABC quilts are perfect for babies! I remember my son would spend countless hours staring at the bright colors and designs associated with the letters. As he learned to talk, I would point to a letter and he would shout out its name, proud of his accomplishment.

—F.A.

1985

Kate's ABC Quilt

Size: 38 x 47" (.95 x 1.2 m)

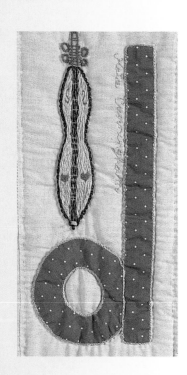

Designers & Organizers: Katie Cunningham and Libby Woodruff
Recipient: Kate Schroeder, daughter of Janice Coverdale and Lou Schroeder

THIS LOVELY QUILT FEATURES SOFT PASTELS with a predominance of turquoise and aqua. Squares and rectangles in a variety of sizes add interest (and make this piece rather challenging to plan and piece). The X block shows a Raggedy Ann doll having an X-ray. Raggedy used to have shaggy red-yarn hair, but as the quilt hung on the wall by Kate's crib, the hair was all "loved" off.

Maggie's Cats Quilt *1985*

Size: 39 x 50" (1 x 1.3 m)

Libby designed the quilt, and we chose cats in a garden scene because of all the cats Judy and Smithy had in and around their house. Maggie was born into this animal environment with Smithy telling a lot of funny cat stories. —S.A.

I remember that Sue came to me with the idea and some cat patterns. We began to sketch some other elements like a tree into the picture for the cats to interact with. This brought about little parts with birds and birdhouses, frogs and lizards, flowers and insects! —L.W.

Designers & Organizers: Libby Woodruff and Susan Adams
Recipient: Maggie Welder, daughter of Smithy and Judy Welder

THIS IS ANOTHER EXAMPLE OF A JIGSAW-PUZZLE assembly put together in horizontal sections, with lots of embroidery and appliqué. Note that only one of our group has been bold enough to plan these challenging pictorial quilts!

1986

Adams' Friendship Quilt

Size: 78 x 80" (1.8 x 1.9 m)

Designer & Organizer: Vicki Skemp
Recipients: Bob and Susan Adams

THIS IS ONE OF OUR MOST AMBITIOUS early projects, calling for skill in piecing, appliqué, and quilting. It is well suited to many different levels of experience: the checkerboard blocks are easily pieced by beginners, the appliqué blocks call for careful stitching, and the center requires one dedicated needleworker to do a lot of appliqué. For variety, use the single Irish-Chain without the appliqué, with a different appliqué, or with embroidery.

I was completely surprised

to know my quilt had been made without my getting any hints. The day of the party was normal for me. We pulled up to Smithy and Judy's house, and I immediately knew what was happening. Then I saw a quilt hanging on the shed. I was overjoyed! My mom had asked me a hundred times when would I ever get a quilt. After about 30 minutes, I called my mom to tell her about the quilt. —S.A.

I cut the green squares one by one using a transparent template in order to center a little pink flower in each square. Tedious, but I think the final effect is worth it. —V.S.

1986

Big Two-Sided Quilt

Size: 78 x 94" (1.8 x 2.3 m)

Designer & Organizer: Vicki Skemp
Recipient: Betty T. Anderson

THIS WAS OUR FIRST quilt-as-you-go venture. This type of quilt is made with blocks that have been quilted before the quilt is assembled. Every block can have a pattern on each side, giving you the opportunity to make a reversible quilt.

Quilt-as-you-go has advantages and disadvantages for group quilting. To the good, people can do all the piecing and quilting at home at their own convenience, which is very useful in a group of people with full-time jobs. On the other hand, the fellowship of the quilting bee is missing, not to mention all that good gossip.

Furthermore, the tedious stitching together of the completed blocks usually falls to the organizer alone. This is absolutely no fun, particularly if, as often happens, people quilt their blocks all the way to the edge instead of leaving the requested half inch free for the seam allowance that is needed for sewing the blocks together. Despite all these potential drawbacks, it is still nice to be able to make a reversible quilt.

An intricate pattern is built up from our minds through our hands into layers of cloth. —A.A.

1986

Dillon's Shoofly

Size: 43 x 44" (1 x 1.1 m)

I was very touched by the beauty of it. —G.K.

The finished products are arrangements of colors, forms, and rhythms put together in a manner that would affect anyones's sense of beauty. —L.B.

Designers & Organizers: Vicki Skemp and Louise Langsner
Recipient: Dillon Wyatt, son of Ginny Koranek and Danny Wyatt

SHOOFLY IS AN ABSOLUTELY TERRIFIC PATTERN for inexperienced quilters. This quilt uses strong Amish-inspired colors—red, green, and purple—with prints chosen by the individual participant. Since the blocks for this quilt are set on point, the construction of this quilt is slightly more complex than Rosie's Shoofly on page 41.

1987

Peebles' Farm Wall Hanging

Size: 33 x 53" (.8 x 1.2 m)

Designers & Organizers: Libby Woodruff and Peggy Barnes
Recipients: Jane and Robert Peebles

THIS IS A PICTURE QUILT designed to represent the recipients' farm. The designer drew the overall design on several sheets of freezer paper that she taped together. Then the pattern was divided, and each person was given a section to embroider or appliqué. The completed sections were returned to the organizers, who then pieced the picture together.

Peggy wanted to make a quilt
that would reflect the scenery looking out from Robert and Jane's farm, so we drew the whole picture out on paper first and then made up "kits" for each person with their part of the picture and the labeled fabrics to be used in their square. I remember thinking that it would be a miracle if all these pieces came back and would fit together just right...miraculously, they did! —L.W.

Peggy's party was on a Sunday afternoon, and I was surprised that my friend Joyce from Raleigh would choose to hang around for the party when she needed to get back for work on Monday. Little did I realize that Joyce knew all about the surprise, had even done a square. —J.P.

Spinning Spools

Roxann and Steve

moved to this area in the early 1980s and jumped into full community involvement. How-ever, many people didn't get to know them until their second child was on the way, so we made them two baby quilts. There was a lot of love in the stitching. —L.W.

Size: 48 x 63" (1.2 x 1.6 m)

Organizer: Doreen Shealy
Recipient: Nicole Rotundo, daughter of Roxann Colwell and Steve Rotundo

THIS DESIGN, from a Georgia Bonesteel pattern, has motion, making it appealing for a baby's quilt. The ruffle makes it unusual and pretty—perfect for a little girl. Our group hasn't always had the luxury of knowing in advance the sex of the little recipient; this time we took advantage of it!

1987

Sailboats

Size: 46 x 47" (1.14 x 1.17 m)

Designers & Organizers: Libby Woodruff and Susan Adams
Recipient: Ryan Rotundo, son of Roxann Colwell and Steve Rotundo

TWO STRONG BLOCK DESIGNS that work well together were used for this baby boy's quilt. The colors and design give a light and free feeling to this piece. It is a good matching of fabric to project.

Receiving a community quilt is such a powerful memory for me. It resurfaces at times of straightening the quilts as they lie on my children's beds. I received both my children's quilts at the same time. I was truly brought to tears, since we had just moved to the area and really didn't know people in the community. It was the sense of caring and the expression of inclusion and acceptance that came from the gift. —R.C.

The fabric in the pinwheels was from Bob's grandmother's collection. The white fabric with baseball players was fabric she had made the grandsons pajamas from. —S.A.

1987

Texas Quilt

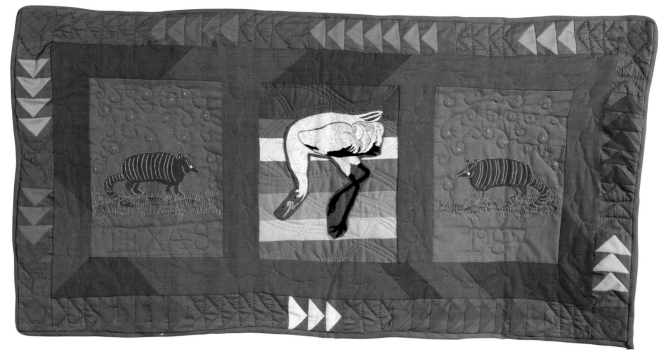

Designer & Organizer: Vicki Skemp
Recipients: Smithy and Judy Welder

Size: 18 x 36" (.5 x .9 m)

QUILTS DON'T HAVE TO BE BED-SIZED—a small wall hanging can serve as a nice remembrance or thank you gift. Three of us made this quilt after spending a week with the recipients on their family's amazing ranch. The ranch is on a major flyway, and we did a lot of bird-watching while there. For this reason, there is a whooping crane embroidered in the center, the border is the Wild Goose Chase pattern, and there are bird tracks quilted in the solid red border. The hanging also features armadillos and, of course, stars at night...big and bright—deep in the heart of Texas!.

1989

Barnes–Parker Quilt

Size: 93 x 93" (2.3 x 2.3 m)

Designer & Organizer: Libby Woodruff
Recipients: Peggy Barnes and Jerry Parker

THIS QUILT PROVIDES an interesting combination of different blocks that produce an overall wreath effect. The soft pastel palette is especially attractive.

By using a pattern of Clay's Choice alternating with a Nine Patch, the center part of the quilt was formed. A wide border for some heart quilting and then more patterned squares on the outside of that with a finished border would make the quilt large enough for their king-size bed. Some of the fabric was polished cotton, which had not been used in many of our previous quilts. —L.W.

1991

Kate Amberg's Quilt

Jane and I designed a (large) baby quilt for Kate Amberg—a long time coming. We got a little elaborate on the quilting design in the center. We copied a design off an antique ceramic tile that my great aunt gave me. I've made three quilts on my own since then. It's not as much fun. —C.R.

Receiving the quilt really gave me a feeling of acceptance and belonging to a strong community. I knew the work involved, and felt a lot of love for those involved in making the quilt. —L.S.

Size: 59 x 70" (1.5 x 1.7 m)

Designers & Organizers: Candace Rice and Jane Peebles
Recipient: Kate Amberg, daughter of Leslie Stilwell and Rob Amberg

THREE DIFFERENT BLOCKS COMBINE in this pretty quilt for a little girl. The organizers washed the fabrics repeatedly before cutting to give the finished product a mellow softness. Intricate quilting fills the center oval.

1992

Susan's Fortieth Birthday Memento

Size: 12 x 16" (30 x 40 cm)

Designers & Organizers: Karol Kavaya and Vicki Skemp
Recipient: Susan Adams

JUST TWO QUILTERS WORKED on this tiny crazy quilt. The traditional corner fans bear the names of the recipient's husband and two sons; the center has her monogram. Beads, lace, ribbons, gold cord, as well as the traditional fancy embroidery, decorate this little remembrance.

This little jewel
was again a total surprise. I still sit and rediscover the small personal details that were beautifully embroidered into the velvets and satins. I'm glad it is behind glass to preserve it for years to come. —S.A.

1992

Log Cabin Variation

Size: 80 x 96" (1.9 x 2.4 m)

Designer & Organizers: Karol Kavaya, Vicki Skemp, Susan Adams, and Libby Woodruff
Recipients: Jane and David Renfroe

THE INSPIRATION FOR THIS STRIKING QUILT, a black-and-white photo in a quilting magazine, featured painted flowers in the central velveteen squares. For our project, the designers specified embroidered flowers.

Since the recipients are both artists, the designers wanted to make a strong visual statement. They chose to work with the sophisticated jewel tones that the wife usually wears. Three of us went to a giant fabric store and indulged ourselves in a veritable buying orgy, choosing sumptuous velveteen and polished cottons.

This quilt gave us a perfect opportunity to try something different in the assembly stage of quiltmaking. Four women got together for a whole day. One of them is a superb seamstress; one has a talent for sorting out angles and placement; the other two are confident about color choices and combinations.

In a short time, we had a two-story assembly line going. We chose colors, cut strips, and laid the pieces for each quilt block on small cushions in correct placement for sewing. One woman carefully carried the cushions upstairs to the seamstress who could easily see how they were to be sewn. By the time the "runner" came back downstairs, another block-on-a-cushion would be ready for her to carry up. We sewed all 20 blocks together this way—they all came out correctly, and we had fun doing it.

Next, we asked each needleworker to embroider a wildflower on the central square of green velveteen. This was a real challenge; it was hard to embroider on the material, and we never did find a marking tool that made a thin, lasting line. Small groups would gather to embroider and to give each other encouragement and motivation to press on.

When the blocks were returned, their beauty struck us. One participant, an accomplished painter, made her first attempt at embroidery, producing the black-eyed Susan. Amazing. The quilt, with its rich colors, beautiful needlework, and strong design, is one of everybody's favorites. At the quilt presentation party, one of the husbands loudly proclaimed, "That's the most visually aggressive quilt I've ever seen!"

Although the quilting is simple, there is so much of it that it took months to finish. We pass quilts around to be quilted at houses where (we hope) several nearby women can work on them. When it came to our house, my husband set the quilting frame up in one of our barns. It was during the fall, and I remember how much I enjoyed going out to work on the quilt. Then I realized I'd spent many hours on it and all I could see was the vast area that remained unquilted. Vicki Skemp came over one day when I was working alone and gave me a big boost by quilting for hours and convincing me that the quilt would eventually get finished. (That was not the only time she gave me the encouragement to finish a needlework project.) —K.K.

1992

House Quilt

Size 91 x 91" (2.3 x 2.3 m)

Designers & Organizers: Vicki Skemp and Susan Adams
Recipients: Richard McCracken and Kathy Hendricks

THIS WAS ONE OF THE MOST FUN TO WORK ON of all our quilts. It was made for a real estate broker and a house builder when they were moving into the old house they were (and still are) renovating. The old School House pattern seemed appropriate. Since one of the recipients has a real affinity for antiques and fabrics from the 1920s and '30s, original and reproduction feedsack fabric was used.

The blocks were pieced together in several sessions by six to eight people working from a cache of old and new fabrics. We had a wonderful time finding prints that looked like roofing material, shrubbery, and windows. We found eyelet and lace for curtains, tiny buttons for doorknobs—we were giddy with the flow of creativity as we constructed "our houses." Most of us have spent many years working on our real homes and gardens, and there was something immensely satisfying about the rapid completion of these perfect little houses.

Next, the house blocks (with batting and backing) went to other participants to be embellished with embroidery that would depict the details of the home—tile, slate, trees, animals, vines, and flowers. People responded enthusiastically: a cat on the roof, a dog in the window, a weeping willow, a kerosene lamp. One block included a tractor, a woodpile, and carpenter's tools.

When the embellishments were finished, the quilters sandwiched the batting between the top and the backing and basted their blocks, then proceeded to decorate the blocks with quilting. Imaginations kept working! The quilting was used to define shingles, clouds, and wind. The participants returned the house blocks to one organizer who assembled the quilt in the usual quilt-as-you-go manner. She alternated the house blocks with plain blue blocks that had been quilted in a simple design by other participants.

Absolute amazement that the secret had been kept from me, and total awe, and then a feeling of filling up with love—from all our friends and especially the women—you know who you are—that put it together initially just for us. Richard always points out "his" square with the tools when we show it to people. The use of the old flour sack material saved for years by my special friend Grace Henderson is a detail of my quilt that still makes me cry. —K.H.

1993

Woodruff Crazy Quilt

Size: 96 x 97" (2.4 x 2.45 m)

Designers & Organizers: Vicki Skemp and Susan Adams
Recipients: Jim and Libby Woodruff

LIBBY HAS BEEN ONE OF THE MOST INDEFATIGABLE and invaluable of quilters over the years. Creative, highly skilled, generous with her time, able to fix other people's goofs, she is a bulwark for our circle of quilters. When it came time to make a friendship quilt for her and her husband, the group wanted to pull out all the stops and produce a real masterpiece.

The organizers opted for a crazy quilt to show off the embroidery skills of our group, with a wide border to highlight fine quilting. Silks, satins, and velvets in colors to complement the recipients' bedroom were the fabrics of choice.

The four corner blocks contain fans, three dedicated to their children, and the fourth embroidered with the name of our county and the date of the quilt presentation. The central block has the names of the recipients embroidered in beautiful satin-stitch script; that much was planned.

For the other blocks, participants were given bits of fabric in the chosen colors, told to use them, add in others, and embellish to their hearts' content. Weekly sewing sessions were held for those who needed help with piecing or embroidery. Egged on by others, people grew ever more bold and creative. "Too busy? Oh, no, put some more beads on. Do you need some of my sequins?" Bits of old silk nightgowns, wedding lace, treasured scraps of favorite dresses, all made their way into this needlework extravaganza.

When I received Libby Woodruff's square, I'm sure my directions said to go for gaudy. That was the year of the big ice storm. We couldn't get out of the door for over a week. Now, it's a strange thing that happens when you work on one piece for a long time. I believe that "perspective" is all relative. The longer we were iced in, for example, the more empty space kept popping up on my square. —F.A.

1993

Jubilee

Libby designed the quilt, including the templates. I did all the sewing. It was especially fun planning this one because it was for only one person–hence the feminine colors and the floral design. —S.A.

Sue and I worked together on this project. I had wanted to work with curved shapes, so I designed this rose and leaf pat- tern. Now Vicki would have something fussy and feminine to hang in her sewing room! —L.W.

Poor Sue! She practically had to twist my arm to get me to come to a birthday luncheon at her house. The warmth and affection I felt when my friends gave me this magnificent quilt will always be with me. —V.S.

Jack Cheney, a bachelor friend, once quilted with us and asked "So, you've done wedding quilts and baby quilts. What's next, menopause quilts?"

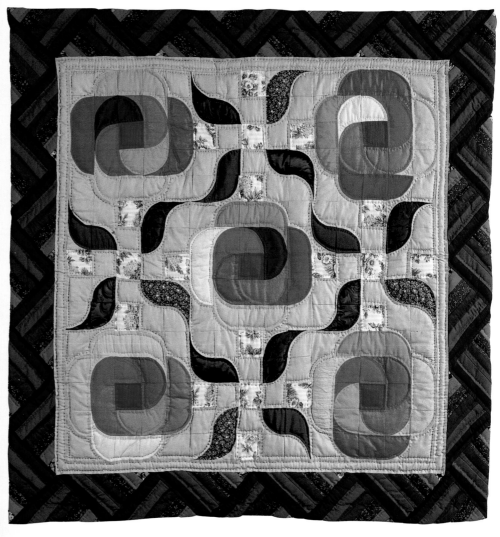

Size: 37 x 37" (.92 x.92 m)

Designers & Organizers: Susan Adams and Libby Woodruff
Recipient: Vicki Skemp

THIS WAS A 50TH-BIRTHDAY SURPRISE designed and organized by two of our group's best seamstresses. Jubilee features strong color choices and an unusual strip- pieced border. The many curves make this a quilt for experienced seamstresses.

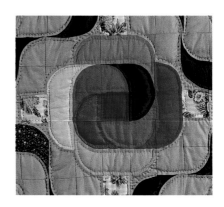

1994

Kendal's Celestial Baby Blocks

Size: 35 x 38" (.9 x .95 m)

Designers & Organizers: Vicki Skemp and Peggy Barnes
Recipient: Kendal Kulp, son of Cindi and Kajur Kulp

Second thoughts
from the designer:
*The pyramid looks a little
lonely against the background.
Now I think I would add
vari-colored streamers coiling
about in the sky.* —V.S.

THE DESIGNER USED A VARIATION of the Baby Block pattern, "stacking" the blocks in a pyramid and then appliquéing the pyramid to a starry-sky background. Since color placement was important, the diamonds that create the blocks were precut by the designer and put into kits. Participants were assigned letters to represent in their blocks and were encouraged to add other motifs in the remaining two diamonds.

After the designer appliquéd the complete pyramid to the background, she tacked down by hand a thin gold cord to outline the individual blocks. The narrow outer border is made from strips of various harmonious solids pieced together on the diagonal. This quilt requires embroidery skills and a competent seamstress to assemble the finished blocks.

1994

Stars

Size: 73 x 90" (1.8 x 2.2 m)

Designer & Organizer: Karol Kavaya
Recipients: Jane and Robert Peebles

THE RECIPIENTS OF THIS QUILT had gotten married before moving to Madison County and had their daughter before we started quilting, so they didn't get a quilt for those occasions. In 1993 they finished building their dream house. A friendship quilt seemed in order.

The husband is an excellent craftsman and has built a house of serene beauty. The designer planned a quilt to complement its simplicity. Since she thought they would prefer a traditional quilt, she chose a star pattern. The quilt is cheerful and magical because of the stars and their fabrics. The use of a deep solid-colored background and the abundant wreath and feather quilting make it elegant.

I had a lot of control over this quilt, choosing all colors and fabrics. My husband cut out all the pieces with a rotary cutter, and we gave "kits" out to be sewn together by the quilters.

When the finished blocks were returned, I was undecided about which of two colors to use for the background so Vicki and I took all the blocks and laid them out on a big piece of blue fabric on her bed. Then we took them and tried them against a piece of unbleached muslin. After deciding to use the blue, I sewed the blocks together, added the wide borders, and we began the quilting in earnest. We tried so hard to surprise them; if they ever guessed the truth, they were kind enough not to let me know. —K.K.

When I think of all that must have gone into making and presenting this quilt, I think about how hard it must have been for Karol to go ahead with the party plans while preparing for an upcoming surgery. But the quilt was/is so beautiful, and the party was full of "good vibes," and the surgery was successful, and it's all connected. —J.P.

Guatemalan Courthouse Steps

Size: 91 x 96" (2.2 x 2.4 m)

Designers & Organizers: Vicki Skemp and Susan Adams
Recipients: Judy and Smithy Welder

Four people assembled this quilt top. Using rotary cutters and two sewing machines, they finished the 20 blocks made of Guatemalan fabric strips in record time. You could, of course, put the fabric into kits and distribute them for completion. However, over the years we have found it's quicker for a few motivated people to work on an easily pieced top than wait for 20 people to get their blocks together and return them. Besides, most people enjoy socializing over the quilting more than working alone on the piecing.

Once the blocks were together, a wide border of mottled-rose fabric, outlined on either side by a thin black strip, calmed the quilt. A narrow border of random lengths of the Guatemalan material and the quilt top was complete but for the final binding of black bias tape. The designers decided to quilt the center with the old-timey fan pattern for two reasons. The recipient had been heard to say that she liked quilting patterns that didn't follow the pieced pattern (a hint at her unconventional nature—a wild woman if there ever was one!), and because any fancy quilting would be lost in the loose weave and complex patterns of the Guatemalan fabric.

The fan quilting was big and fast, no need for tiny, perfect stitches, and everyone enjoyed themselves. The rose-colored border was another story; here the stitches would show and the weave design was executed with care. This would be a good project for a group of beginning quilters, especially if there are one or two with some experience.

The idea for what kind of quilt to make for a person or couple can be reached by various routes. When I saw an advertisement using wildly colored, geometrically patterned upholstery fabrics put together in the courthouse steps pattern, I immediately thought of Judy, who loves bright colors and wild designs. I tore out the ad and squirreled it away in my idea notebook. Several years later when we decided it was time to make a friendship quilt for the Welders, I showed the picture to some of Judy's other friends. Everyone agreed that this looked right. We took into consideration the purple carpet and rose-colored dust ruffle already in their bedroom and decided to use mostly Guatemalan fabrics, as we knew that Judy, a weaver, was particularly fond of them. —V.S.

I remember the enormous outrush of love and excitement, the festive spirit, the celebration of friendship. —J.W.

1995

Jenny's Flowers

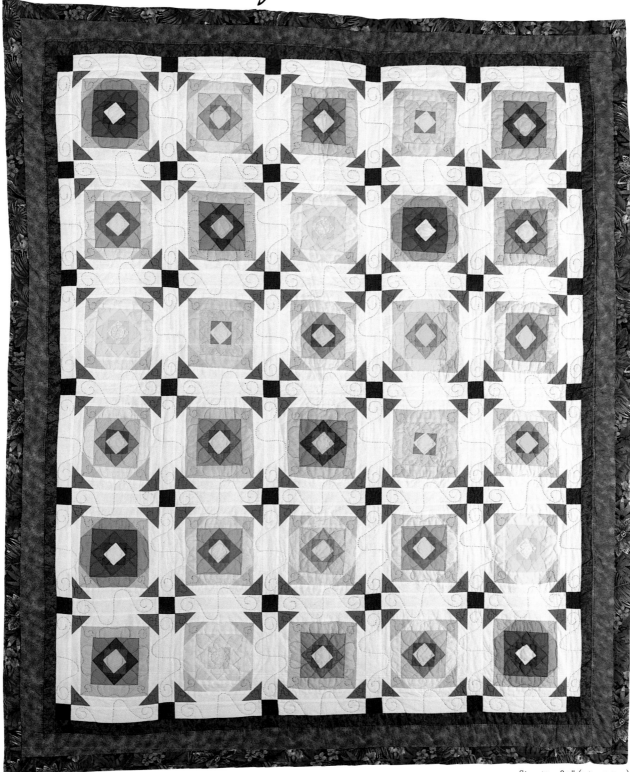

Size: 71 x 80" (1.7 x 1.9 m)

Designers & Organizers: Libby Woodruff and Jennifer Woodruff
Recipient: Jennifer Woodruff

THE BEAT GOES ON...! When 18-year-old Jennifer Woodruff told her mother she wanted to make a quilt, we felt we were moving into the next generation. Jenny's mother has been one of the driving forces of our group since the beginning, and Jenny has inherited her mother's love of quilting, color, and intricate piecing.

When my oldest daughter Jennifer was a senior in high school, I wanted to make her a quilt for her graduation gift. At some point in the process she took over and began to call it "her" quilt and "her" project. Being the good mother that I am, I just let her do it.

I just had to keep her on schedule so that she would get it done before the end of the year. But alas, time was running out and we needed help on the quilting part. So I called some of my trusty quilters. In three long days it was nearly done, so Jennifer and I finished the last of it just before she went off for her freshman year of college! —L.W.

1996

Ryan's Nine Patch

Try not to spend six hours in the fabric store coming up with the perfect design! —C.K.

Size: 46 x 50" (1.1 x 1.3 m)

Designers & Organizers: Cindi Kulp and Ruth Uffelman
Recipient: Ryan Horrell, son of Clifton and Mary Beth Horrell

A GROUP OF YOUNG MOTHERS, most of whom had not done much quilting, produced this lively hanging using bright contemporary fabrics to bring a fresh new look to the reliable old Nine Patch.

1998

Marcia and Charlie's Wedding Quilt

Size: 85 x 85" (2.1 x 2.1 m)

Designers & Organizers: Libby Woodruff and Candace Rice
Recipients: Marcia Schneider and Charles Pfaff

THIS QUILT IS A NON-TRADITIONAL LOG CABIN variation. Contemporary fabrics were used in subtle shadings with an emphasis on purples and greens.

Candace bought the fabric and washed it all before we got together. We had planned to do a Log Cabin design, so it was just a matter of cutting the fabric for each kit, and getting the kits out to all of their friends. It was rewarding to make a warm quilt for their "shower" gift and to rejoice in their new-found love! —L.W.

Amish Crown of Thorns

Size: 91 x 91" (2.3 x 2.3 m)

Designer & Organizer: Vicki Skemp
Recipients: Drew and Louise Langsner

THE UNUSUAL CHOICE OF COLORS WAS ENVISIONED as suiting the pale floors and poplar log walls of the recipients' handmade cabin. The pattern is an easy one to assemble and leaves room for lots of nice quilting.

It is full of colors that I love and covered with patterns of tiny stitches that leave me awestruck when I think of the many hours my friends spent sewing. Being given such a wonderful quilt is overwhelming. It is like being wrapped in love and joy. Living with this quilt and sleeping under its warmth is like a nightly blessing and a daily reminder of the gift of friendship. When I look at our quilt I think about how much like patchwork our community of friends is. We are all so different—like the various fabrics stitched together to make a quilt. Sometimes you can't imagine a certain piece fitting in, sometimes the effect is startling, and sometimes pieces have to be rearranged to get harmony; but somehow it all works and the overall design is beautiful. —L.L.

1999

Crazy ABC

Size: 52 x 52" (1.3 x 1.3 m)

Designer & Organizer: Vicki Skemp
Recipient: Fay Lilia Knight, daughter of Charley and Barbara Knight

THIS BRILLIANT EXPLOSION OF COLOR was made for a two-year-old recently adopted in China. The designer planned it as a tool to help the child learn English. She also pieced all the blocks, then many of them were distributed to be embellished by others. The loving stitches of fanciful embroidery make this quilt a bright decoration and a heartfelt welcome for a new child.

Starry Night

Size: 74 x 92" (1.8 x 2.2 m)

Designers & Organizers: Karol Kavaya and Vicki Skemp
Recipient: Friends of Madison County Library

STARRY NIGHT WAS CREATED FOR THIS BOOK and donated to the Friends of the Madison County Library to be raffled as a fund-raiser for a new library building. The pinwheels are executed in several different blues and purples to add vibrancy and depth to the background. Can you find one pinwheel in which the fabrics are unique?

Organizing a Group Quilt

The quilts were a way and a reason to connect. We came together with a multitude of motives: to identify a worthy recipient (often there were too many reasons to do a quilt, too many babies, too many life events); to plan and organize; to cut and compile the quilting packets; to create the directions (writing legible and workable instructions has not always come naturally); to distribute packets. Then there were the phone calls to check on progress, seeing each other to turn in completed squares, and the inevitable—finding those who had not finished. The traditional quilting get-togethers also happened, to piece or join the tops of squares, to quilt, or to sew the already lap-quilted squares (together), and to finish the quilt. —P.B.

What follows is a synopsis of twenty-odd (some, very odd) years of experience in making group quilts. During that time we have worked with rank beginners, skilled fiber artists, and everyone in between, to create quilts both plain and fancy in all sizes. We have tried to distill the knowledge gained from these varied experiences in order to pass along to you ideas, systems, and patterns that have worked well for us. We have also remembered our past mistakes and problems in the hope that we can help you avoid certain pitfalls. Though every group and each quilt will be different, we believe these time-tested methods will be useful to anyone beginning this exciting and rewarding endeavor.

The Organizer, or, Somebody Has to Be the Bad Guy

The quilters had just presented a beautiful wedding quilt to friends immediately after their ceremony. As one of the bride's friends was enjoying gazing at the quilt she had organized, filled with the lovely sense of a job well done, the husband of one of the other quilters came up to her.

"You all have really done a good job! What does it take to put something like this together?"

"Well, you kind of have to keep after people to make sure they get their stuff done on time, and then you have to make sure everyone gets a chance to quilt..."

"Somebody has to be the bad guy, huh?"

Select an Organizer

The organizer is the one who will see the quilt through from beginning to end, delegating work where possible, filling in the gaps when necessary. The organizer is usually, though not always, the person who has the idea to make a quilt for a certain event and is, therefore, the one laden with the most responsibility. She is the one who makes sure all jobs get done. Ideally, the organizer has some sewing skills, or has a good friend who can provide this help.

The organizer may be the one who plans the quilt. Then she contacts the potential participants, purchases the fabric, and assembles and distributes the kits for the blocks. She needs to call and remind people to get their blocks finished, assembles the completed blocks into a quilt top, and prepares the top for quilting.

She may host, or get others to host, quilting bees. She makes sure the quilting gets done on time, binds the edge of the quilt, and sees that a party is planned to present the finished masterpiece. The organizer doesn't have to do all these things herself. With any luck, she will find responsible helpers among her quilting friends.

If you are making a group quilt for the first time, we advise it be a team endeavor. Most of our quilts have had one or two organizers. Once you have a pool of experienced organizers, they can easily work together with first timers who then become organizers-in-training.

Once when I was in charge of a particular quilt, the blocks were very slow in coming back. A few weeks past the deadline I was shopping in a local hardware store, and, from the corner of my eye, saw a woman whose block was not yet returned slip quietly out of sight behind a nail bin. No one likes to be nagged or to do the nagging, but sometimes it's in the job description for the organizer. —V.S.

...of course this was the night before the due date. (Although I was not the hider in Bowman's!) —C.R.

Keep up the communication. Share the work. —L.B.

Keep enough contact

so that the project can be completed on time; be prepared to beg, be prepared to fix a block that comes back to you wrong. Buy enough fabric. Have enough commitment from others when you start the project to see it through (sometimes that means a few very dedicated people). Provide complete kits. Give clear instructions. Give accurately cut pieces of fabric so no one has to curse you when they're at their machine. Assure them it's all right to call with questions. When they get weary, remind them how much the quilt will mean to the recipients. When you ask for a certain size block, tell them that a ¼ inch variation is allowed. —K.K.

Make sure that all instructions are clearly given, even for experienced quilters, because not everyone does things the same way. I have given instructions that all seams should be ¼ inch and even explained how to measure that on the sewing machine...and still gotten back ten different sized squares from twenty people. The bottom line is to have fun and spend time with good friends in a special communal effort! —L.W.

Making a Group Quilt Step-by-Step

Establish a Time Frame, or, She's Having a Baby!

You want to make a group quilt, and you have a recipient in mind. Now what? First, think time frame. No matter what kind of quilt you are planning, you should have some general date of completion in mind.

A wedding quilt, anniversary quilt, or going-away quilt provides its own logical date of presentation. A friendship quilt, one done "just because," can be timed to suit the organizer. For a baby quilt, ask yourself if you want to present the quilt to the expectant mother, or to the mother and the new baby. We generally opt for the latter, because, in part, it provides us with an opportunity to meet the newest member of our community, but mostly because it gives us extra time to work on the quilt!

Remember, in setting your deadline allow plenty of time for all steps. Be especially mindful of the deadline for getting the pieced blocks back from the participants. We find that the more time you give participants to complete the blocks, the more time people will take; the sadly human tendency to procrastinate is alive and well among quilters.

In general, we think it is a good rule to allow participants no less than two weeks for completing and returning an easy pieced block, and no more than six weeks for a difficult block involving fine embroidery. When you give participants more time than that, blocks seem to get forgotten, lost, or eaten by the dog. The organizer should also allow herself a generous buffer zone of time that is allotted to calling (and hassling, if necessary) people who haven't returned their blocks.

You will also need to factor in time for sewing the blocks for the top together, for basting the top, batting, and backing together, and especially for quilting. Don't forget to allow time for binding the edge and for sewing on an optional sleeve and I.D. panel. (Too often, we have done these final tasks in the dark-thirty hours on the morning of the surprise party.)

The most important thing is to be realistic! Make sure that each person is willing to help and that they can meet the time lines. Be prepared to call and double check on them if they pass the time schedule. If time is not critical, this isn't so important, but the project may only be the priority that you are willing to make it. —L.W.

STEP 2

Contact and Enlist Participants

Your next concern is to determine how many folks are willing to work on the quilt. Contact all the friends and relatives of the recipient who you think may be interested in your project. If you wish, include out-of-town people. Working long distance has the potential for added aggravation, but it can be very special for the recipient if you include close friends and relatives in this way.

When talking with potential participants, try to get some idea of their skill level—can they piece a block by hand or on the sewing machine, can they quilt, embroider, appliqué, or are they willing to learn? Can they get the work done on time, or are they planning to be in Nepal for the next six months?

Remember that your goal is to be as inclusive as possible and to give everyone who wants to participate a chance to help in some way. Occasionally, we've had people who are totally unable to sew give money to help with the cost of the materials, thereby entitling them to have their names on a quilt as a participant.

STEP 3

Choose Your Design

All quilts are made from individual blocks that are pieced together to make the quilt top. Sometimes one person will do several blocks, sometimes two people will work on one. Sometimes people will not do a block, but will help with the quilting.

The number of participants for your quilt and their skill levels will directly influence your design choice. We have done baby quilts with only nine or ten participants, and bed quilts with as many as 40. We have even done a few small wall hangings with only two or three participants.

Once you have a fair understanding of the group with whom you'll be working, you can begin to design your quilt. We generally begin by first deciding on the size of the quilt, whether it will be a square or rectangle, and the number of blocks it will contain. When deciding on the size of your quilt, keep the standard sizes of batting in mind:

Crib	45 by 60 inches	(1.1 x 1.6 m)
Twin	72 by 90 inches	(1.8 x 2.2 m)
Full	81 by 96 inches	(2 x 2.4 m)
Queen	90 by 108 inches	(2.2 x 2.7 m)
King	120 by 120 inches	(3 x 3 m).

The batting should be approximately 3 inches (7.5 cm) larger on each side than your quilt top.

The following illustrations offer some basic ideas you can use for designing your quilt.

As shown in figures 1a, b, and c, you can add to a quilt's size, within reason, by adding a border.

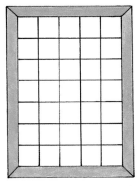

Fig. 1a. Border with mitered corners

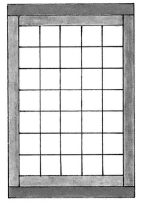

Fig. 1b. Border made with strips of fabric

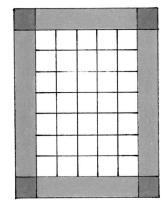

Fig. 1c. Border with blocks at the corners

Notice in figures 2a and b, that if you are alternating two patterns or colors in your blocks, and you want to end up with corners that are the same, you will need to use an uneven number of blocks up and down. We usually opt for the uneven number, feeling that it results in a more pleasing balanced look.

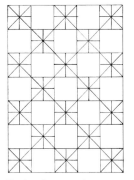

Fig. 2a. Corners that are the same

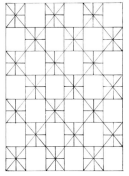

Fig. 2b. Corners that are different

When designing a quilt, one of the things you'll have to decide is the placement of the blocks. Figures 3a and b show two examples. Will they be separated from one another by solid blocks or sashing, or will they be sewn directly to each other? Simple blocks look fine when they are next to each other. More complex or fancy blocks look good when separated by plain blocks or sashing. Sashing forms a sort of frame around the individual blocks and also lessens the number of pieced blocks needed to achieve a given size quilt.

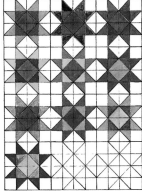

Fig. 3a. Simple blocks next to each other

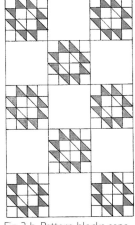

Fig. 3 b. Pattern blocks separated by plain blocks

As shown in figures 4a and b, you will need to decide whether to place each block "on point" or "square."

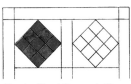

Fig. 4a. Block "on point"

Fig. 4b. Block positioned "square"

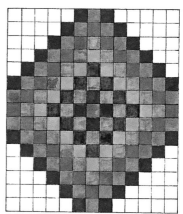

Fig. 5a. One Patch

Thinking About Your Design

In addition to taking into consideration the skill levels of the participants, consider the personal tastes of the recipient (or the recipient's parents in the case of a baby quilt). Sometimes it just takes thinking about the recipient and imagining what he or she might like. (It helps to look around their home, if possible.) Sometimes the designer already has a pattern or motif she's been itching to use.

Colors are usually chosen to reflect the recipient's (or the designer's) taste, and sometimes people are simply seduced by fabrics they see in the store. If you don't know a person's taste, a traditional pattern in traditional colors is usually a safe choice. (For more color ideas see page 92.)

What Makes a Design Easy?

In picking a geometric quilt pattern, look for one using few pieces worked in straight lines. Unless you are working with fairly good seamstresses, avoid choosing designs with curves; that way lies potential frustration and heartbreak.

Squares are very simple, and a one-patch, four-patch, or nine-patch design (see figs. 5a, b, and c) is perfect for beginners or quilters in a hurry. An Irish Chain (see

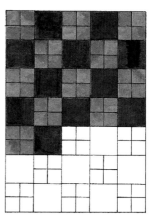

Fig. 5b. Four Patch

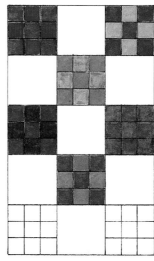

Fig. 5c:. Nine Patch

fig. 6) can be extremely elegant and still very easy to accomplish. Triangles aren't difficult to work unless their points are long and thin with stretchy bias edges. Shoofly (see fig. 7) is a personal favorite of ours, as is Ohio Star (see fig. 8). Pinwheel (see fig. 9)

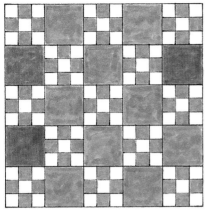

Fig. 6. Irish Chain

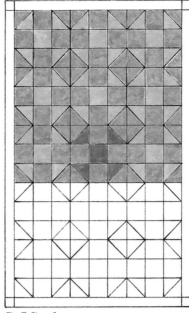

Fig. 7. Shoofly

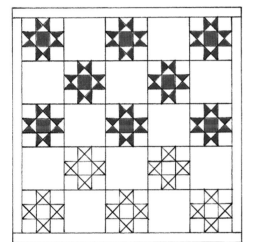

Fig. 8. Ohio Star

Fig. 9. Pinwheel

is another pattern suitable for first-time needleworkers.

As a rule of thumb, the fewer the pieces and seams in a patchwork block, the less chance there is for error and for size variation. However, be prepared for variations on the returned blocks. Though you instruct your participants to sew with ¼-inch (.5 cm) seams, you'll be amazed at how differently people measure the same ¼ inch.

One of the simplest solutions for a group of mostly inexperienced participants is to use squares or rectangles of a background fabric on which each quilter embroiders or appliqués a design. Then the blocks are joined together using a simple sashing. (See figs. 10a and b.)

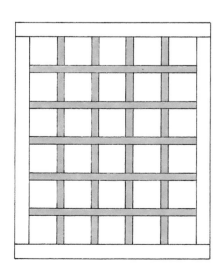

Fig. 10a. Plain block joined by simple sashing

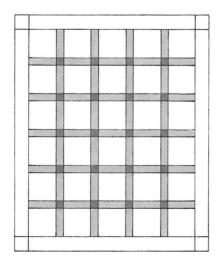

Fig. 10b. Blocks joined by decorative, pieced sashing

Choose Your Quilting Pattern

Now is the time to consider quilting patterns. You can wait until the top is complete for a final decision; but if you know that you want to feature the quilting, be sure that your quilt's design incorporates sufficient areas of solid colors or subtle monochrome prints to show off your careful stitching. On the other hand, "busy" fabric will camouflage uneven stitches. Think about your group's abilities, and plan accordingly.

The simplest choice for a quilting pattern is outline quilting (see figs. 11a and b), where you stitch around an image or around the elements of a pieced pattern. The quilting is usually done either ¼ inch (.5 cm) away from the seamline or "in the ditch," which is in the seamline itself. Another traditional approach suitable for beginners is an allover quilting pattern. This can be superimposed on a simple pieced pattern and provides an exciting counterpoint (see fig. 12).

But if your idea of quilting runs to fancy wreaths and feather plumes, cable borders and Celtic knots, visit a quilt store and see what they have to offer in the way of templates. They are the easiest way we have found for marking a quilt with a beautiful pattern, and the templates make it possible to re-mark lines easily if your pattern becomes hard to see. If you have a template you know you want to use, make sure that there are suitably sized areas in the quilt design to accommodate the template's size.

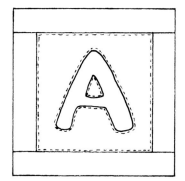

Fig. 11a. Outline quilting on an appliquéd block

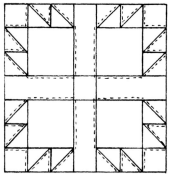

Fig. 11b. Outline quilting on a pieced block

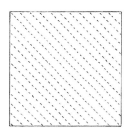
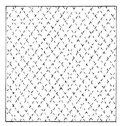
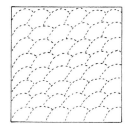

Fig. 12. Allover quilting. *Left to right:* diagonal, diamond, and clamshell

RANDOM PLACEMENT AND MAVERICK SQUARES

Sometimes we deliberately choose to vary a quilt design simply by using fabric that is almost, but not quite, like the others. We like to imagine an old-timey quiltmaker who has used up all of one particular fabric in her scrap bag and has had to substitute something similar.

Another trick is to make a "mistake" in putting together a block. For example, in a quilt of nine-patch blocks, if your pattern calls for five darks and four lights, one or two blocks with four darks and five lights can look more interesting.

Even though these mistakes are not always readily apparent at first or even second glance, a quilt with a few such "errors" can be more visually interesting and more alive than a quilt that repeats itself with machinelike precision.

Choose Fabric, Batting, Backing, and Binding

FABRIC

After you've chosen your quilt design, unless it is to be a scrap quilt where the participants choose their own fabrics, you will need to select the fabric. If you know the recipient's color preferences or wish to coordinate the quilt with the decor of their home, your color choices will be obvious and easy to make. Otherwise, the organizers get to pick the colors they like! It helps to have someone with a good eye for color combinations be part of the decision-making process at the store. We advise that no more than three women go to the store to choose fabric—more than that is cumbersome, since too many personal tastes get into the mix.

Use 100 percent cotton fabric. You'll be putting a great deal of time and work into this project, so be care-

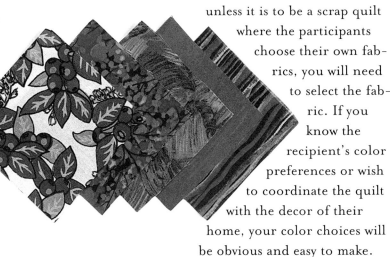

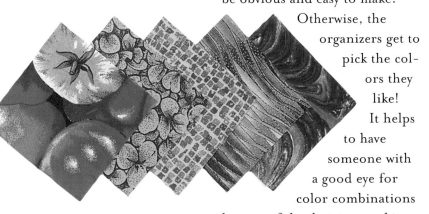

Play with fabric scraps or samples until you find a combination that is pleasing.

ful with imported fabrics, since they may not be colorfast. Also avoid "bargain" fabrics that may be flimsy, may have too much sizing, or may run when washed. We like to buy a little extra fabric to allow for miscalculations or disasters. ("Mikey put my quilt pieces in the blender! Can I have another kit?") This may be one of the reasons some of our organizers have amassed such a collection of scraps.

Remember that your quilting stitches will show more clearly on solid-colored fabric. If you are not sure of the quilting skills of the participants, choose prints that will mask uneven stitches.

BATTING, BACKING, AND BINDING

You may choose to buy your batting, backing, and binding when you purchase your fabric, or later, if desired. Since we live an hour away from any good fabric stores, we often try to do all our shopping at once.

Furthermore, if you buy these items when you purchase your fabric, it will give you a better idea of your expenses. This is an important consideration if you are asking participants to contribute toward the cost of material for the quilt.

Batting

A look at your fabric store or quilting catalogue will reveal a dazzling array of batting—polyfill, cotton, silk, wool, and blends in a range of sizes and prices. Our personal preference is for a low loft (not too fat and puffy), which allows the quilting stitches to show well.

We have not had a good experience with 100 percent cotton batting, finding it difficult to needle, though there are newer versions that promise easier

quilting. Avoid the cheapest polyester batts; the fibers can migrate through the fabric of your quilt, producing an unpleasantly hairy look. Our favorite batting, though slightly pricey, is a blend of cotton batting with 20 percent polyester.

Read the instructions that come with your batting and follow them carefully, especially if you must prewash your batting. Note also quilting directions; some batting calls for very close quilting to keep it in place, others need far less. For the standard batting sizes, see Step 3, Choose Your Design, on page 84.

How Wide is 45 Inches?

When determining fabric yardage, remember that so-called 45-inch (1.1 m) fabric may not actually measure 45 inches across, even as it comes straight off the bolt. Plus, the fabric may shrink when you prewash it. Also, we recommend that you remove the selvages before use. For these reasons, we figure our yardage based on an assumed usable fabric width of 40 to 43 inches (1 to 1.15 m).

Backing

If your quilt top is 100 percent cotton, your backing should be the same. In choosing your backing, be sure to select fabric that, while not flimsy, is easy to needle. A large bedsheet, though tempting because of its size, is usually difficult to quilt because its material is so closely woven.

Though reason tells you that the backing should be measured to the same size as the finished top, the fact is that the quilting sometimes draws up the backing fabric. For this reason, we allow a generous extra 3 to 5 inches (7.5 to 12.5 cm) per side when buying backing fabric. Believe us, it's worth the extra expense to avoid the sinking feeling that comes when you realize, near the end of your quilting, that your backing isn't quite reaching the edge, and that you somehow have to piece a strip onto it. Also, if you think you will hang your quilt on the wall, buy enough extra backing fabric to make a sleeve on the back of your quilt to accommodate a hanging rod (see Step 21, Finishing Touches, on page 117).

Determining the Amount of Backing

For a small quilt that is 30 inches (76 cm) wide or less, a single length of standard 45-inch-wide (1.1 m) fabric will be ample. A larger or wider quilt will require piecing the back (see step 13, Prepare the Backing, on page 109) or using wider fabric that is especially intended for quilt backing. Since the selection of colors and prints in the wider fabrics is quite limited, you may want to piece the back in order to achieve the look you desire.

If your quilt is 70 inches (1.7 m) wide or less, multiply the length of the quilt by two. Now add 1 yard (.9 m) to allow for the extra 5 inches (12.5 cm) per side and fabric for a sleeve for hanging the quilt. Note: If you choose not to have a sleeve, 20 inches (51 cm) extra will be adequate.

If your quilt is more than 70 inches (1.7 m) wide, you will need three lengths of material. For example, if your quilt is 76 x 90 inches (1.9 x 2.2 m), you will require 300 inches or approximately 9 yards (8.1 m) of fabric plus ¼ yard (23 cm) for your sleeve.

When we were beginning quilters, we often opted for a busy print for our backing so that the unevenness of our stitches (usually worse on the back) wouldn't show. As we became surer of our quilting skills, we sometimes chose a solid backing in a color that contrasted with the top and allowed the quilt to be displayed on either side.

Binding

When we first began to make quilts, we did as many old-timey quilters did and simply made our backing a few inches larger all around. When the quilting was finished, we pulled the backing up around the quilt's edge, then turned it under and blind stitched it into place on the quilt top. Over time, we learned that using a bias strip rounds the corners more smoothly and also wears much better. We've seen older quilts using the backing-as-binding method in which the only worn places were along the edge. Now we recommend bias binding.

While many experienced quilters prefer to make their own bias binding for a custom look, we usually choose to buy packaged single or double-fold bias binding. It comes in many colors, is easy to use, and is usually packaged in 3-yard (2.7 m) lengths. When figuring the amount you need, remember to add extra for joining lengths and for corners. You can buy the binding when you purchase your fabric, or wait until the top is pieced or even until it's quilted.

For some quilts, an unobtrusive color of binding that matches and blends with the border may be preferable, while other quilts may demand the little jolt of color that a contrasting binding can provide. Since

binding is one of the last steps, you may find that it is easier to make this final design choice once you've completed all the quilting.

Prepare the Top and Backing Fabric

Note: This applies only to cotton fabric, not to silks, satins, woolens, velvets, or certain specialty fabrics used in quilts that you do not intend to wash.

When you get your new fabric home, first wash it in hot water using the normal setting and your regular detergent. Next, tumble dry the fabric on the hot setting. This should ensure that any shrinking or running of dye will take place before you piece the quilt. Tear off the selvage edges to avoid any temptation of using them—those little printed words or white bands won't look good on your quilt top. Finally, iron your fabric, since marking or rotary cutting is more accurate on a smooth surface.

EXCEPTION TO THE RULE

There are quilters who prefer the new look and feel of unwashed cotton fabric for its crispness and body. Those working with detailed appliqué often find that unwashed cotton is easier to use. For an art quilt, or any quilt that will never be washed, this is certainly an option.

SPECIALTY FABRICS—USE WITH CARE

Some of us have occasionally used beautiful imported fabrics for wall hangings. We have found that they, particularly batiks, madras, and wood-block prints, are not always colorfast and will bleed. The blue and red dyes seem especially prone to this. Use these specialty fabrics only on pieces that will never be washed. It's heartbreaking to have a piece of work you've spent many hours on be ruined when it is washed and the colors run.

Make the Kits

We believe that we achieve the most consistent results when two or three people cut out all of the pieces for the blocks to be sewn and put them into kits. If this isn't feasible, or the quilt is to be made scrap style, where each worker provides her own fabric, we make templates and send them out with our instructions. In this step we will cover both methods.

PRECUT KITS

These kits will have all the pieces, cut correctly and ready to assemble, for a chosen quilt block. Also included are detailed instructions. To make the kits, the organizer(s), will cut out all pieces for all blocks in the quilt (these can easily number in the hundreds).

If your pattern pieces are squares, triangles, or rectangles, and you are

familiar and comfortable with the use of the rotary cutter, you can speed your cutting and eliminate the step of pencil marking. Otherwise, marking with pencil and using scissors works

just fine. When marking fabric for cutting, we've used two methods: measuring and templates.

MARKING BY MEASURING

We can best explain this by offering an example. If you're making a Nine-Patch (a quilt block made of nine equal squares) or a Pinwheel (all triangles), you can use a straightedge to mark a straight line along the selvage edge of the fabric (having first remembered to remove the selvage as instructed in step 6). With a metal or a plastic square, mark a perpendicular line along the adjoining edge. Now you can work with a 90° angle and straight lines (see fig. 13). Using a ruler you can measure and mark your fabric at the correct intervals (e.g., 3½ inch [9 cm] intervals across each edge). Then, connect your marks and you will have your squares ready for cutting (see figs.14a and b on page 97).

90°

Figure 13

You can mark triangles in this same manner. First, determine the size of square that will produce two triangles of the desired size. Then be sure to mark the diagonal at the exact corner, as shown in figure 15, to achieve triangles of identical size.

Figure 15

Note: If you want to cut triangles from a square (and we do), measure the length of one triangle leg (one of the shorter triangle sides). Add ⅞ inch (2.2 cm) to that measurement and cut a square that size.

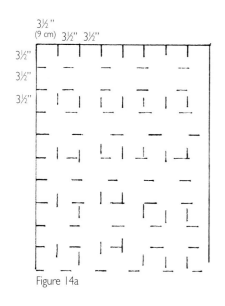

Figure 14a

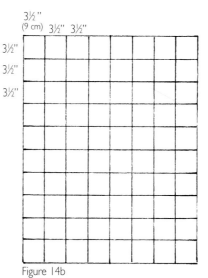

Figure 14b

MARKING BY TEMPLATE

You will be repeatedly placing the template on the fabric and tracing around it. (Yes, this is slow....but so meditative.) Use a shared line wherever possible and try to get the most out of your fabric (see fig. 16).

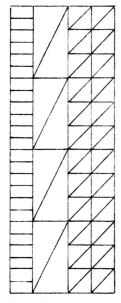

Figure 16

TIPS FOR MARKING AND CUTTING

Be extremely careful in all your marking and cutting. Always try to hold your pencil at the same angle. Always cut on the line, not to one side or the other. It's best to not do your marking and cutting when you're feeling rushed. Seemingly minute errors, when multiplied many times, can mean trouble later on. A key difference between a quilt made by one person and a quilt made by a group is that when one person does all the marking, cutting, and sewing, you're assured of more overall consistency.

Note: Your templates and/or precut pieces should include a ¼-inch (.5 cm) seam allowance on all sides of each piece. Please remember to include this allowance when marking the fabric or making a template. If some of your participants will be sewing by hand, instruct them to measure an exact ¼ inch (.5 cm) from each edge, then mark this sewing guideline with a pencil.

TEMPLATE KITS

These kits will contain templates and instructions. They may include the fabric to be used or they may ask that the participants provide some or all of their own.

MAKING YOUR OWN TEMPLATES

You can easily make your own templates. If you are using templates from a book or other source, trace your template shapes onto clear plastic template material (this is our recommended choice, which is readily available at craft or quilting shops) or thin cardboard or poster board (this is economical, but templates made from these materials tend to wear away and lose precision with much use).

If you are designing your own pattern, first draft a precise pattern on paper. Remember to include the ¼-inch (.5 cm) seam allowance on all sides of each piece. Next, transfer the various pieces of the pattern to your template material. Use a sharp pencil to make a thin, clear line. For maximum precision, hold the pencil as near to vertical as is comfortable.

Mark your template with an arrow showing where the straight grain of the fabric needs to be on each piece (see fig. 17). Tip: When marking triangles with a template, you can avoid stretchy bias edges by placing the edge of the triangle that will be on the outside of the block on the straight of the grain (see figs. 18a and b).

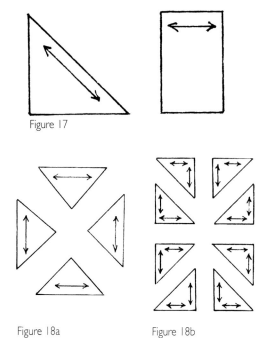

Figure 17

Figure 18a   Figure 18b

When you cut out your template, be as accurate as possible. Use a good sharp pair of scissors and cut on the line, not to one side or the other. Write the pattern name, letter of the piece, and size of the finished block on each template—this is helpful when using the templates again. A final optional touch is the use of a product such as gritty dots that you stick on your template to keep it from sliding around on the fabric when you are marking your shapes.

ASSEMBLING THE KITS

Now that you've cut out your quilt pieces or made your templates, the next step is to assemble the kits. The kits will contain the instructions and the correct pieces needed to complete the assigned block. When all the kits are assembled, double-check them to make sure each one contains what it should.

Always save some extra templates and extra fabric. (You did get extra fabric, didn't you?) Inevitably you will need replacements—a kit will have been lost in the mail; or you will get back a block so badly done that you will choose to make a new one.

Write your instructions for the least-skilled non-quilter you can imagine—in other words, the more detail the better. Remember, what is obvious to you may not be obvious to another. When you have completed writing the instructions, have someone else read them, checking for clarity. Don't omit this important step or you could have many phone calls from confused quilters. Experience has taught us to try to avoid the sheepish feeling we get from handing out incomplete or unclear instructions.

To help you write your own instructions, we've provided the guidelines below. Don't be discouraged by this lengthy list. We have tried to anticipate all the problems you may encounter. Of course, if your workers won't read or don't follow the instructions, they will have trouble, but you, at least, will have done your part. Right?

Remember and remind your participants (and yourself) that making a quilt is not a life or death matter. Most mistakes can be fixed, and your goal is not a perfect quilt but a quilt made with love and joy (and at least some attention to detail).

INSTRUCTION GUIDELINES

I. On the *outside* of the envelope containing your kit, tell your participant to immediately check the contents to make sure all needed pieces are included.

2. Begin your instructions with an inventory of what should be in the kit and how many blocks the participant is being asked to make.

3. Give the name and provide a sketch of the block(s) to be done, including the size.

4. Make a color chart, if necessary (see fig. 19).

5. Provide the recipient's name. If the quilt is to be a surprise, note that in BIG LETTERS.

■ green
▨ blue
▩ red
⊡ yellow
☐ muslin

Figure 19

6. Include notes on the ¼-inch (.5 cm) seam allowance. (See the General Instructions on page 121.)

7. If necessary, provide instructions to handsewers on marking a sewing line that is ¼ inch (.5 cm) from the raw edge.

8. Explain the importance of pressing, not ironing, at each step, and of pressing the seam allowances to the dark-fabric side. (See the General Instructions on page 121.)

9. If each block is to be signed, include instructions for this. Embroidery or indelible ink are good choices. Indicate to the participant where you want the signature placed on the block (see fig. 20).

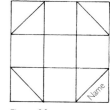

Figure 20

10. Include a diagram for assembly and order of procedure, with instructions to measure at each step and redo if necessary. (See Organizer's Instructions on page 133.)

11. Remind participant to avoid stretching the pieces if they need to remove or pick stitches from badly sewn units. Taking apart and resewing the unit too many times can damage the fabric.

12. Did we mention the importance of the ¼-inch (.5 cm) seam allowance? If you are working with people who sew clothing, they may be accustomed to a ⅝-inch (1.6 cm) seam allowance. Stress, and stress again, that the pieces for the quilt use a ¼-inch (.5 cm) seam allowance!

13. Tell participants to press and measure the finished block. Remind them of the exact size of the block. If necessary, note any allowable variation, e.g., that ¼ inch (.5 cm) smaller or larger is okay.

14. Include the deadline for returning the block.

15. Include the address for returning the block.

16. Provide phone numbers for a help line, giving the participants people to call if they need help with the block.

17. If known, give the date of the quilt presentation and any party plans.

18. Request money to help pay for quilt materials. (We only ask for small amounts based on the cost for that quilt.)

PREPARING FOR THE NEXT STEP

Your kits have gone forth. Aside from sewing together your own block or blocks, you can breathe easily for a few weeks until it's time to start getting the finished blocks back. Or you may want to use the time to help some novice seamstresses to sew together their blocks. A get-together for your beginners may solve a lot of problems, as nothing replaces hands-on help for the inexperienced.

Shoofly block in process of assembly.

What I like so much about the community quiltmaking is how it lets everyone contribute. It doesn't matter if you don't have great talent or skill at design or sewing, you can still be part of making a beautiful piece of art. An important aspect of the quilting process for me is how it allows us all to focus on the people or event that the quilt is honoring and celebrating. When I'm working on my block, I think about the person it is for and what they mean to me and how our lives have touched. Being part of the quilt circle lets me feel more connected to the person(s) who will receive it, because I am joining with other friends who are all putting their appreciation and love into the quilt. —L.L.

The Blocks Come Back

One of the most exciting parts of group quiltmaking is when the blocks start to come in. With special blocks involving appliqué, embroidery, crazy quilting or quilter's choice, it's fun to see what the needleworkers' imagination and skill have produced. There is curiosity as to whether the seamstresses did their job well, and great joy when that's the case. And, there's disappointment when there's a serious goof—or should we say, a challenge? (See below, How to Fix Blocks That Need Fixing.)

Be aware that you may have to make some tearful or threatening phone calls before all the blocks are returned. Since making reminder phone calls is much easier than begging, don't wait more than a couple of days after the deadline to contact the errant participants. Occasionally we've had to ask that a block be returned, finished or not, so that we can get on with assembly of the top. Usually though, we've planned ahead and set a deadline with a buffer zone, which allows us to be patient and wait for all finished blocks to be returned.

Once all the blocks are completed and returned, your first job is to press and measure each one. In a perfect world, if you asked for 8½-inch (21.5 cm) blocks, that's what you'd get. But it's not a perfect world and human error can affect measuring, marking, cutting, and piecing. One way or another, we've dealt with every block that has come back to us in the past 20-something years. Most of them have been just fine; others have required various fixes.

HOW TO FIX BLOCKS THAT NEED FIXING

This section includes some of the most common problems you will encounter with the block and how to fix them. If none of these fixes are appropriate for your problem blocks, you will need to make a new block, using that extra fabric you should have on hand.

The Block Is Too Big

If you can do it without affecting the pattern, trim each edge to obtain the desired size. (**Note:** As an example, this will work for Pinwheel blocks, but not for Shoofly blocks.) See figures 21a and b.

The Block Is Too Small

If the block is no more than ¼ inch (.5 cm) off, use a pin to mark the edge with the incorrect seam allowance. This will remind you to use a ⅛-inch (.3 cm) seam allowance when joining it to another block. (See step 10 on page 106, for joining instructions.)

If the block is off by ½ inch (1.5 cm) or more, you can try to sew strips of fabric to the edges to reach the desired size. This works best if you have some fabric that matches the overall background of the offending block.

OH NO, IT'S NOT PERFECT!!
Karol's Story

Note: *I'm telling the following story to help you avoid the low feeling that may come when, try as you might, blocks, even your own, are not the exact dimensions you were hoping they might be. But if they're not, there is a multitude of things you can do to deal with them. And then you can move on. You can make the quilt and enjoy the giving of it, and look forward to the time when you can do it again.*

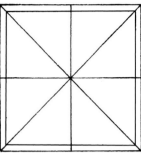

Fig. 21a. Pinwheel

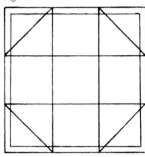

Fig. 21b. Shoofly

It was a Saturday morning in January. Snow was falling lightly when I stepped out of my house and headed to Vicki's. During the 30-minute drive I was not comforted—the snow had increased in intensity. Once there, we eagerly went up to her sewing room, ironed our new fabric, and cut out the pieces to make a sample block. It wasn't until the final pressing and measuring that surprise and dismay struck. The block was not the right size! It was off by ¼ inch (.5 cm). We thought we'd been careful but had to evaluate our steps to try to find where our problem lay.

Vicki had the idea to change some measurements and see if our block would come out the correct size this time. Again we ironed fabric and cut pieces to make a block. Taking a little more time, Vicki sewed it together. Still not right.

I looked out the windows to a view made white by the incessant snow. I sat down, weary and discouraged. Why couldn't we make a perfect block? After a silent couple of minutes, I said, "This isn't about perfection."

Vicki looked at me and said, "Nope" (or something to that effect).

It was a revelation. When I realized and accepted that even when using correct measurements, good tools, attention to accuracy, and a focused mind, the result may be other than perfect, I was able to relax. This endeavor is NOT about perfection; it is about creativity, imagination, a combined effort toward a common goal, working with others, the spirit of giving, love, friendship, generosity—you get the picture.

After some restful minutes, we stood up, went over to the work table, and proceeded to cut most of our fabric into strips, getting a good start on our quilt. I put a stack of fabric into my bag, ate a warm bowl of soup by the fireplace, and set off for home. With four inches of new snow on the winding roads, the going was *very* slow. But with little traffic (other than a hound dog that insisted on running alongside my car for two miles) I made it safely home on a quiet winter afternoon.

That's what it's all about.

BE PREPARED

If you organize a quilt, be prepared for the unexpected. Once, a participant was given a red background block and asked to embroider a tree on it. (The color and image have been changed to avoid embarrassment!) She returned her work on time, but she had embroidered the tree on a flimsy piece of organdy, and returned the unused red background fabric. Since all the other background blocks were red, and since organdy wasn't sufficiently durable for a baby quilt, the organizer decided to cut out the embroidered tree and appliquéd it to the red background. We never asked and never learned the reason for this misunderstanding.

Decide on the Layout

If you are following a predetermined layout, such as our pattern for the Starry Night quilt on page 128, you will sew your blocks together according to the given pattern. If you have chosen a random or scrap pattern, lay all your blocks on the floor or on a bed where you can look at them and shift them around to balance the colors (or unbalance them) to your liking. As shown in figures 22 and 23, different effects can be achieved with different color placements.

Fig. 22. Positioning the same Maple-Leaf block in different ways provides a variety of effects

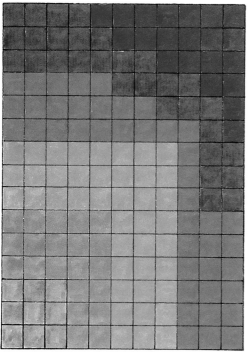 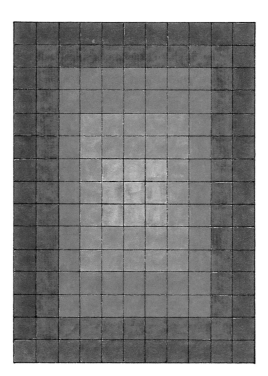

Fig. 23. Two different effects using a One-Patch pattern

Sew the Top Together

After you've decided on your quilt's layout, stack each row of blocks in the correct order, left to right, with the leftmost block on top. Pin a label with the row's number on each stack of blocks. This will help you keep your place in case your sewing is interrupted.

Use a ⅛-inch (3 cm) seam allowance when joining a slightly smaller block to a standard-size block

Sew the blocks together one row at a time, using ¼-inch (.5 cm) seam allowances. If you had some blocks marked with pins because the seam allowance was too small, now is the time to make that correction. (See step 8, How to Fix Blocks That Need Fixing on page 103.) Leave the labels on the left-hand block of each row to avoid getting the rows mixed up.

Press all seams on the top row to the left, the next row to the

right, and so on, alternating all the way down. Now sew these long strips together, matching up your seams between blocks as best you can, pinning along the way as shown in figure 24. Press the long seams that join the rows all the same way—up or down, it doesn't matter.

If you have chosen to use sashing in your quilt, assemble the top in the same manner, always being careful to match seams with those on the other side of the sashing, eyeballing as best you can. (See fig. 25.)

BORDER OPTIONS

If your quilt design incorporates borders, it is time to add them after you've sewn the top together. Non-pieced borders (i.e., solid strips of fabric) are an easy way to add size to your quilt and can provide a nice background for fancy quilting.

Before you cut your borders, measure your quilt. Suppose you planned it to be 72 by 94 inches (1.75 x 2.2 m), but as you measure the four sides, you find that each opposing side is slightly different. Do not cut your borders to these different lengths; rather, find the average of each pair. As an example, if one side is 73 inches (1.8 m) and the opposite is 71 inches (1.7 m), cut your two borders to 72 inches (1.75 m).

Ease the border fabric on the longer side, and pull it to fit on the shorter. It is particularly important that opposite borders be the same length if the quilt is to hang on the wall. If the quilt is to be on a bed, some size variation would not be as obvious.

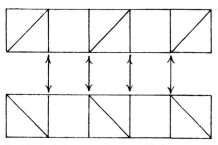

Fig. 24. Match the seams between blocks

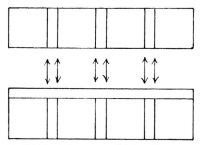

Fig. 25. Match the seams of the sashing

Press and Mark the Top

After the top is sewn together, you will need to press it carefully and completely. This will be your last chance to do so. Take this time to look for forgotten pins. Check all your seams for any gaps, and repair them. Find the center of each of the four sides of your quilt, and mark each center with a safety pin at the edge of the quilt. This will help you align the top with the backing when it is time to put your three layers together.

There are varying opinions about marking the quilt with the quilting pattern at this stage. It's certainly easier to mark your design before it goes on the frame; this provides the advantage of marking a single layer of fabric on a hard surface. If you've chosen an allover quilting pattern that you cannot mark with masking tape (see Masking Tape Hints below), then you will need to mark the quilt now.

If you will be using a stencil to execute smaller designs block by block, you may want to wait to mark the quilt when it is on the frame. Since some quilting markers tend to wear off as the quilt is handled, the markings often need to be redone while quilting. For this reason, some quilters always wait until it is on the frame to mark the quilt.

If you will be doing only outline or in-the-ditch quilting, you will not need to mark the quilt. Similarly, if you are using only straight lines in your quilting, these can be marked as you go with masking tape. For example, we did not mark our Starry Night quilt on page 128 at this stage. Once the quilt was on the frame, we used masking tape as a sewing guide for the straight lines.

MASKING TAPE HINTS

Apply masking tape to the quilt only after the quilt is on the frame. Since the tape can leave a sticky residue which is hard to remove, never leave the masking tape on the quilt overnight. Also, buy new masking tape to use for quilting. The yellowed old roll lurking in the toolbox or in the back of the kitchen drawer is far more likely to leave dreaded residue than a nice fresh roll.

QUILT MARKERS

You can purchase a variety of quilt markers for your top.

• Blue, water-soluble, felt-tip markers provide good clear lines that don't rub off and they vanish when dabbed with cold water. Since some authorities warn that the ink may deteriorate the fabric over a long period of time, it may be best to leave the ink on your quilt as short a time as possible. Occasionally we have found that the ink is difficult to remove entirely.

• Purple vanishing markers contain an ink that vanishes within 24 hours, sometimes much sooner. This is not suitable for marking your quilt ahead. Like all felt markers, it dries up sooner than you think it should.

• Quilt-marking pencils can be used to mark the quilt on or off the frame. They tend to wear off with handling. Most, but not all, are easy to remove completely when quilting is done. They are vexing to sharpen, since they have a tendency to crumble. Unlike felt-tip markers, they do not dry up.

• Hard-lead pencils (#3 or #4) make a thin clear line that can be mostly hidden with close quilting stitches. Their lines are hard to see and follow on dark or busy fabrics. They can be used to mark the top before it is layered with the batting and backing.

Step 12

Prepare the Batting

Read the manufacturer's instructions that come with your batting. Some batting needs to be prewashed. Follow the directions *exactly*. (They mean it when they say "don't agitate," as we have found to our sorrow!)

If your batting doesn't need pre-washing, it's a good idea to open it up, spread it out on a bed, and smooth out the wrinkles. Let it relax for a few hours and it will be easier to deal with. (Aren't we all?)

Step 13

Prepare the Backing

You should have already washed the backing fabric, removed its selvages, and ironed it as directed in step 6 on page 95. Measure your finished quilt top. As stated in step 5, you should have enough backing to extend 3 to 5 inches (7.5 to 12.5 cm) on each side of the top to accommodate the drawing up of the backing that happens when the layers are quilted together.

Unless you are making a small quilt (less than 34 inches [60 cm] wide), or are using the extra-wide fabric made especially for quilt backing, you will have to piece your backing. The three most usual ways of doing this (see fig. 26) are: two equal lengths of fabric joined by a vertical center seam; or, three equals lengths of fabric consisting of one central panel, with strips of equal width on either side. The latter is made by taking two equal lengths of fabric, cutting one of them vertically down the middle, then sewing the resulting two strips to either side of the panel that is intact. Though the center-panel method may

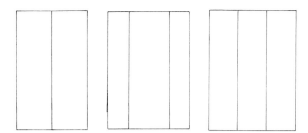

Fig. 26. Three ways of piecing the backing

seem like more trouble, it provides a better looking reverse side to the quilt. Also, if this applies to you, quilt-show judges are said to prefer the center-panel method.

If your quilt is as wide as 120 inches (2.8 m), you will need to sew together three panels of 45-inch (1.1 m) to achieve this width.

Once you have sewn your backing together, iron the seam(s) open, which will make for a little less bulk when quilting. Then press the entire piece. Find the centers of each side, and mark the edge there with a safety pin. This will help with alignment in the next step.

Step 14

Layer the Top, Batting, and Backing

For many years we did our layering and basting on the floor with our rear ends high in the air. Now some of us have large cutting, dining, or Ping-Pong tables that allow us to work in more comfort and with considerably more dignity. Karol still bastes on the floor. "I just try to do it when no one else is home. It's sort of hard on the knees but I have a table that's only big enough for baby quilts."

Whichever you use, floor or table, the first step is to lay down the backing, wrong side up, and secure its edges with masking tape. The backing should be stretched out gently so there are no wrinkles, but should not be under tension. If you're working on

the floor, secure the backing edges at intervals all around. If using a table, center the backing. Depending on the relative sizes of your quilt and your table, there may be no tabletop showing. In this case, gravity will keep the several layers where they belong.

Next, gently lay your batting on top of the backing, smoothing out any wrinkles. The batting should be 3 inches (7.5 cm) larger on each side than the quilt top. Like the backing, it can get drawn up in the quilting process. Now place your quilt top, right side up, on these two layers. Center it on all four sides using the safety pins placed in steps 11 and 13 for aligning the top and backing.

It is helpful to work with another person. You can each gently tug on the batting from opposite sides to make sure it's free of wrinkles. Often, if you gently run your hands over the surface of the quilt, from the center outward, you can feel and smooth out minor wrinkles in the batting. It may take a little adjustment before you're confident that all three layers are lying as smoothly as possible and that you've correctly aligned them. Note: Don't hurry this step.

Helpful Hint: Rough hands can catch the batting and move it all over the place. Use hand lotion, making sure to apply it ahead of time so your hands won't be sticky when you begin work.

Baste the Three Layers Together

Using a long needle and a thread that is easy to see on the quilt top, begin in the center and baste through all three layers with $\frac{1}{2}$ to 2-inch-long (1.3 to 5 cm) stitches. Following a basting pattern similar to the one shown in figure 27 should suffice for most full-size quilts.

As you baste along toward the edge, smooth any wrinkles toward the edge. Occasionally check the back of the quilt to make sure there are no wrinkles. If there are, take out your basting and baste again. Finally, baste all four outer edges.

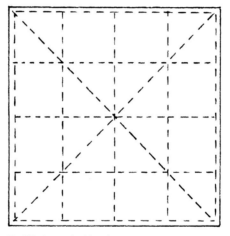

Fig. 27. A standard basting pattern

BASTING WITH SAFETY PINS

For small quilts, baby quilts, and wall hangings, we sometimes use medium-sized safety pins instead of basting stitches. Safety pins are quicker to use and are easier to redo if you find a wrinkle. We have never used them for larger quilts, fearing that we could damage the quilt top when the quilt remains rolled on the quilting frame for a long time.

Set Up the Quilting Frame

A quilting frame with a base which you purchase or build yourself is ideal. You will tack or stitch the top and bottom edges of your quilt to the two longer rails. You will then roll the quilt onto the rails and quilt in sections, rolling the quilt as necessary to expose the unquilted areas.

If you don't have a quilting frame, you can easily make one using four 2 x 2s, four 4-inch (10 cm) or 5-inch (12.5 cm) C-clamps, and four ladderback straight chairs. First cut two of the 2 x 2s into 46-inch (1.2 cm) lengths (or have them cut for you at a lumberyard or home store). Then cut the other two into 98-inch (2.5 m) lengths. These lengths will make a frame that will accommodate quilts up to 86 by 100 inches (2.1 x 2.5 m).

As with a ready-made frame, you will first tack or stitch the quilt to the two longer rails, roll the quilt, then C-clamp the long rails to the two shorter ones, which will rest across the tops of the chairs. This is not the greatest quilting frame, but it has the advantages of being cost effective, easy to make, portable, and easy to store. We have quilted many of our quilts using this type of frame.

QUILTING-FRAME PATTERN

If you are inclined to build things, or have someone to do it for you, here is a dandy frame we have all enjoyed using. It's very solid and works well for a large group of quilters.

You will need:
One 2x4, 10 feet (3 m) long
One 2x6, 6 feet (1.8 m) long
Two 2 x2s, each 8 feet (2.4 m) long
8 carriage bolts

Use a stable lightweight wood, such as a good grade of white pine. (This will make it easier for one person to move the quilt frame around.)

2 rails 86 x 1½ x 1½" (214 x 4 x 4 cm)

30" (76 cm)
21" (53.5 cm)
2 ends
30" (76 cm)
30" (76 cm)

HOOP ALTERNATIVE

If you absolutely have no room to set up a quilting frame, even large quilts can be quilted using hoops. In fact, many quilters prefer using hoops when quilting fancy patterns such as feather plumes and wreaths which involve frequently changing the direction of your stitching. The great big hoops can be tiring to hold and unwieldy unless on a stand. A good size hoop for group work is approximately 14 inches (35.5 cm).

To use hoops with a group, first make sure your quilt is closely basted. Then drape the quilt over a big table and seat the quilters around. Each quilter will have her own hoop. You probably can't seat as many quilters around the quilt at a time as you could with a frame. Each quilter will require extra room, since she will be twisting her hoop around as she works.

STEP 17

Put the Quilt on the Frame
ATTACHING THE QUILT

Cut two strips of fabric, such as cotton, muslin, or lightweight denim, each 6 inches (1.5 cm) wide and almost as long as the longest rails. Fold the strips in half lengthwise. Using a staple gun or thumbtacks, tack one strip along each of the long rails. Make sure you tack the two raw edges to the wood. You will baste your quilt to these strips, the top edge to one strip, the bottom edge to the other. Begin basting in the center; baste to one side, then go back to the center and baste to the other side. Keep the edge you are basting parallel to the rail.

You can omit using the strips. Instead, use thumbtacks to tack the top edge of the quilt directly to one of the long rails, pushing the thumbtacks through all three layers of fabric. If you do this, be sure to place the thumbtacks close to the edge of the quilt where the holes will be hidden by the binding. Start tacking at the center of the rail, then work toward the ends, smoothing the edges as you go. Do the same for the bottom edge of the quilt to fix it to the remaining long rail.

We prefer using the fabric strips. Pushing thumbtacks into wood through the two layers of fabric and batting can be difficult. Putting the strips on the rail is a one-time job, since you will keep the strips on the rails when the quilt is finished and removed. The strips also provide you with the advantage of quilting closer to the ends when the quilt is on the frame.

ROLLING THE QUILT

Once the quilt is attached to the rails, it is helpful to have at least one other person work with you. Not only are you trying to prevent massive wrinkles in the quilt, you are trying to get it wound squarely and evenly on the frame. If one end of the quilt is wound more tightly than the other, the quilt will be off-kilter. An equal amount of quilt on each rail at the start ensures that you can begin quilting in the very center of the quilt. We highly recommend making this a two- or four-person job.

To start, stretch out the quilt that you have attached to the rails—do not pull it taut. Begin rolling toward the center, rolling the quilt under, onto the rails. Keep a steady tension as you roll. When only the central two or three rows of your quilt top are showing, stop rolling and secure one long rail to the two short rails. If your

Quilting
gave me the opportunity to
visit at length with folks—
a rare occurrence. —S.S.

Our spouses or significant
others would have their own
stories to tell about the quilt-
ing bees. How evenings saw
their quiet living room filled
with women and babies.
Dinner might be leftovers,
again, but the guys usually
knew where to find their
C-clamps.—F.A.

quilting frame is one that rests on chairs, secure one long rail to the short rails with two C-clamps. Once one long rail is secured, tightly pull the quilt, then secure the other long rail. You want the quilt to be stretched but not taut; if the quilt is under undue strain, the tension can pull out the stitches.

Place your quilters' chairs around the quilt, and get ready to work. Many of us find we quilt more comfortably if the quilt frame is slightly higher rather than lower, but there are always individual preferences. Sometimes we put the frame in front of a sofa to accommodate the "low" sitters and arrange dining chairs on the other side for the "high" sitters.

Arrange the Quilting Bees

Quilting is a mixture of work and fun. Unless someone really dislikes needlework, the lure of socializing with friends and acquaintances, as well as the promise of good food and drink, will bring people to the quilting frame. A full-size quilt takes many hours to finish, but most people say that the quilting is the most satisfying part of the whole process for them.

First, some planning. Determine how many people can fit comfortably around the quilt when it is on the frame. Usually, for a large quilt, three people per each long side is the most comfortable arrangement. It is seldom possible to quilt at either short end of the frame.

Next, contact your quilters. Give them a choice of different days, then ask them to choose one. Plan both week and weekend days to accommodate a variety of schedules. Don't just say, "Come if you can," or you may end up with too many or too few quilters. Try to get people to commit to the day they've chosen—if they don't show up, there's a space someone else might have filled.

Tell your quilters you plan on working most of the day—our usual plan is 10 a.m. to 4 p.m. with a lunch break. Remember, it takes time to warm up and get into the rhythm of quilting, even for the most experienced quilters. Also, the good stories never get told until later in the day!

We usually ask everyone to bring food to share for lunch; if this is too much trouble or special diets are involved, quilters can bring a bag lunch. The hostess usually provides the beverages. She should also make sure there is plenty of light to quilt by and comfortable seating around the frame. Elbowroom may be a different story!

A few of the items you may need for quilting. *Clockwise from top:* pattern template, masking tape, marker, thread, thimble, finger guard, scissors

The hostess should have these items on hand:

- Extra pairs of small scissors for cutting thread
- Two or three spools of quilting thread in the correct color
- Good-quality quilting needles in two or three sizes
- Adhesive bandages
- A few thimbles (though really everyone should bring her own)
- Masking tape if used for marking
- A spare pair of reading glasses and a needle threader aren't a bad idea if any of your quilters are over 50.

STEP 19

Quilting

The major objective in quilting is to keep the batting from shifting around between the top and bottom fabrics. What we mostly see is the attractive solution to this utilitarian problem—

the stitching pattern on the top of the quilt. Good quilting takes practice, but even beginners can do a respectable job.

To begin, mark your pattern if you haven't done so already (see step 11 on page 108). Buy thread that is specifically designated for quilting. Traditionally, you use the same color thread for all the quilting, but the choice is up to you. If most of your quilters are beginners, you may want to use a color that blends with the background in order to camouflage crooked stitches.

TWO WAYS OF HIDING THE KNOT

Thread your needle with a length of thread that measures approximately the distance from your fingertips to your elbow. Using a longer thread will slow you down. Make a small knot in one end. Push the needle into the quilt top approximately ¼ inch (.5 cm) from where your quilting is to begin. Only go through the batting, then bring the needle up to where the line of quilting is to begin. Pull gently until the knot rests on the surface. Take one or more sharp tugs to pop the knot through the top to hide it in the batting. If your knot pops all the way through, it's too small; if you can't get it into the batting, it's too large.

A second method is to put your threaded needle, knotted on the end, into the quilt from below, pushing up at the spot where you want to begin quilting. As the needle comes out of the top of the quilt, take the needle in your sewing hand pulling it and the thread upward. Pinch the backing fabric directly under your needle, gently pulling the fabric down while pulling the needle and thread up. When your thread is mostly through the quilt,

QUILTER'S KNOT

Thread your needle. With the needle in your right hand (if you're right-handed) and the long end of the thread in your left hand, aim the end of the thread toward the needle and grasp it to the needle with the fingers holding the needle. Wrap the end of the thread around the needle (near the point) three or four times. Continuing to press the wrapped thread with your right-hand fingers, pull the needle and thread all the way through the wrapped thread. You should have a tiny, tidy knot left at the end. Trim any tail.

grasp the thread with your sewing hand near the quilt top, and tug, pulling the knot up into the batting. Again, too large or too small a knot won't work. Look or feel carefully on the quilt's underside to be sure the knot has indeed popped through the backing and does not show on the back.

QUILTING STITCH

For the quilting, you will use a simple running stitch with a single thread. After you have set your knot, begin by inserting the needle straight down. Use the index or middle finger (with thimble if you use one) of the hand on top of the quilt to push the needle through all three layers. Use the underneath index or middle finger to feel whether the needle has penetrated all the layers and to turn it back upwards.

Some quilters use a thimble on the hand that is below the quilt to protect their finger. We find this cumbersome. The under-the-quilt finger does get poked and sore, but eventually it will develop a good quilter's callous.

You will be using a rocking motion, one or two stitches at a time. When you are satisfied with the size and consistency of your stitches, try working three at a time, then four (see fig. 29). It

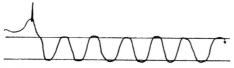

Fig. 29. The quilting stitch

takes a lot of practice; be patient and forgiving with yourself and others. The motion and rhythm of quilting can be very relaxing. Sometimes we listen to music we enjoy if only a few of us are working. Books on tape are good when you are quilting alone.

ENDING THE LINE OF QUILTING

When you've come to the end of quilting, or your thread becomes too short, secure your thread without making a knot. Some people make a double backstitch and hide the remaining thread in the batting. That works, but we prefer the following neater alternative. This is more complicated to explain than it is to do. We encourage you to practice it a few times (see fig. 30). You'll find it's a secure way to end your work.

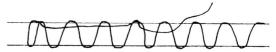

Fig. 30. Alternate ending stitch

Make your next to last stitch. Now take your last stitch, making it a backstitch. Pull your needle and thread to the top at the far end of that stitch, then tuck your needle into the batting in the center (and under the thread) of that stitch.

Using your lower hand to make sure the needle doesn't poke through the back, pass the needle through the batting in the direction you just came from, three stitches back. Come up at the end of that third stitch, and back in and under the thread at its center. Go through the batting approximately 1 inch (2.5cm), then bring up to the surface. Trim your thread end so it won't show.

ROLLING THE QUILT

The center of the quilt should be showing when you first roll the quilt onto the frame. Regardless of the quilt's size, always begin your quilting in the center. First quilt the center row of your pattern. Then, preferably with help, unclamp the frame and roll the quilt toward one end, keeping the tension even. Reclamp the frame, and continue quilting from where you left off.

You will gradually be quilting toward one end of the quilt. Re-roll as often as necessary till you reach the upper or lower end of the quilt. At the end, quilt as close to the edge as you can, while still maintaining a decent stitch.

Now roll the quilt all the way back to the center and quilt toward the other end. When you have done all the quilting that is possible to do on the frame, remove the quilt from the frame and complete any unfinished bits using hoops. At this stage, since the rest of the quilt is already quilted, you may not need to use hoops.

STEP 20

Bind the Quilt

If you happen to have a stash of different color bias tapes, take turns laying different colors along the edge of the almost completed quilt to see which looks best. The effect of this simple detail on a quilt's appearance is substantial. You can also take the unbound quilt to the fabric store to audition different binding colors.

There is no need to prewash packaged binding. Open the binding out, placing the outer fold to the top side of the quilt with right sides together. Sew along the fold line through all three layers of the quilt. This will stabilize the edge and prevent the batting from creeping away from the edge into the body of the quilt. Unless your quilt is very tiny, you will have to piece together several lengths of bias-tape binding. You can sew these together beforehand or add them in as you work your way around the quilt's edge.

As you come to each corner, sew the binding in a gentle curve.

Sew on the fold line through all three layers.

Once the binding is sewn around the entire quilt, fold it over and down around the quilt's edge to the backing. When you turn the quilt over, you should be looking at the right side of the bias tape. Pin the binding to the backing at intervals, then blind stitch it to the quilt. Be sure that you only stitch through the backing and batting. Check the quilt top frequently for stitches that went all the way through. If they show, undo them. Deal with corners as neatly as possible, folding the tape and securing with tiny stitches to create the illusion of a mitered corner on the back.

STEP 21

Finishing Touches

You're almost there! Remove all basting threads, and trim off any stray thread ends. Be careful! At this stage, we've seen overexcited quilters make small holes with the points of their scissors while hurriedly trimming threads. Needing to mend a just-finished quilt is really depressing.

Check once more for forgotten pins or needles. If the quilt has gotten dusty or has collected cat hair (cats *adore* napping on quilts that are on the

Folding the tape and securing it with tiny stitches makes a neat corner.

frame), try tumbling it (the quilt, not the cat) in the dryer on the no-heat setting. Vacuuming with low suction can also help. Of course, if the quilt is actually soiled (blood, sweat, tears), you may need to wash it in the machine (only if the quilt is washable, of course). Use cold water with a mild soap (one made specially for woolens or for quilts) on a gentle cycle. Then tumble dry on low heat.

HANGING SLEEVE

We try to put hanging sleeves on any quilts that may be displayed on a wall. To do this, cut a strip of fabric you've washed and ironed, preferably the same fabric used for the backing. It should be approximately 5 inches (12.5 cm) wide and as long as the width of the quilt. On the two long edges of the strip, turn the ends under approximately ½ inch (1.3 cm), and press or hem. Now turn the shorter edges under, turn them once again so no raw edges show, then hem. Now pin the sleeve to the upper edge of the back of the quilt. Stitch the sleeve to the back of the quilt, just along both long edges of the sleeve (see fig. 31). Your stitches can go through the backing and batting, but you do not want them to show on the quilt top. Check the top as you stitch to be sure this isn't happening. Later you can slip a dowel, stick, or curtain rod through the sleeve to support the quilt when it hangs.

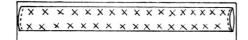

Fig. 31. The hanging sleeve with cross-stitches

IDENTIFICATION PANEL

Please don't omit this step. We did when we first began, and now, 20 years later, there's a lot we don't remember about some of our quilts. We generally use unbleached muslin or pastel cotton, prewashed and ironed, to make our panel. We write with indelible ink, using a fine-point pen intended for marking fabric, first testing the pen on the fabric to make sure it doesn't bleed. Information to include may be the name of the quilt, recipient(s), date of presentation, occasion for the quilt (wedding, birth, etc.), where it was made, name(s) of designer/organizer, and names of all participants.

Make your panel large enough to hold all necessary information. Turn the edges of the panel under and hand-stitch the panel to the bottom of the back of the quilt. Again, don't let your stitches show on the top.

CONGRATULATIONS!!!

Rejoicing and Hurrahing!!! Dancing in the Streets!!! You've finished!!! Put the quilt somewhere you can enjoy looking at it for a while. Right now this may feel like one of your grandest accomplishments, not unlike giving birth. This is a good time to take a picture of the quilt. When you've given it away, you'll be glad to have a record of it.

Planning Your Surprise Presentation

YOUR PARTY PLANS WILL DEPEND ON YOU, your quilters, and your recipients. Since the party is a surprise, do remind your party guests not to leave invitations where the quilt recipients might see them. We present our baby quilts at the end of a regular baby shower. Wedding quilts are presented at the wedding party or at a party scheduled for a later date. We usually reveal friendship quilts at parties ostensibly created for some other purpose than to honor the quilt recipient(s). Surprise! Keep in mind that someone has to make sure the honorees actually show up—you don't want an even bigger surprise!

We often hang the quilt up rather than gift wrap it. This provides for a wonderful shock effect. Furthermore, people are able to enjoy and admire the quilt all through the party.

Then came Steve's and my marriage quilt. Everyone did a great job of keeping it a secret, but I had gone to Roxann's to vaccinate dogs and cats. She had an invite on her fridge for our quilt giving-away party at Tom and Karol's. Oh well—it didn't dampen the surprise of actually seeing it. —C.R.

I didn't suspect that a quilt was being made for us, but I was puzzled when a friend said one day, "I just can't get anything done till I get that quilt off my mind—guilt, I mean guilt off my mind." —V.S.

…Total Surprise! We were four hours late to Sara's Mardi Gras party. Sue led me over to the most beautiful quilt I'd ever seen. She flipped the corner back, and when I saw our names I burst into tears. —J.R.

GIVING SOMETHING BACK

By enclosing a photo of their quilt with each thank you note, the recipients will be giving something back to the quilters who worked on the project.

Simple Patterns Suitable for Group Quilting

HERE ARE PATTERNS FOR THREE quilts with variations. They range from a small quilt with only nine blocks, to an ambitious, bed-covering quilt with 99 pieced blocks.

Each pattern will give the yardage requirements (where applicable), the cutting and piecing instructions, possible variations (ways to make the quilt larger, smaller, simpler, more complicated), as well as quilting suggestions.

General Instructions

Though you should already have read our detailed step-by-step instructions in the previous pages, we want to stress again five important basics:

1. Before you begin to sew, mark your sewing machine so that you will be sewing with a consistent ¼-inch (.5 cm) seam. To mark the machine, place the needle near the down position. With a ruler, measure ¼ inch (.5 cm) from the needle to the right (including the needle in the ¼-inch [.5 cm] measurement.) Place a piece of masking tape on the stitch plate at that measurement, to the right of the measurement. As you sew, you will guide the edge of your fabric along the edge of the masking tape. Practice on a piece of scrap fabric. Sew your seam, take the fabric out of the machine, then measure the seam allowance. It should be just ¼ inch (.5 cm). The stitches of the thread should be on or just inside the ¼-inch (.5 cm) measurement, or what we call a "scant" ¼ inch (.5 cm). Always use an exact ¼ inch (.5 cm) seam allowance.

2. Remember that pressing is different from ironing. With pressing, you use less back and forth movement, which causes the fabric to stretch and will distort your pieces.

3. Press your fabric at each step.

4. Press all seams to the side and toward the darker fabrics where possible. Do not press the seams open, as you would do in dressmaking. (Pressing the backing is an exception to this rule. See Prepare the Backing on page 109.)

5. Note that when we give measurements for cutting strips, we assume the width of your fabric is 40 inches (1 m). It may measure a few inches more and that's fine. Don't bother to cut it down to 40 inches (1 m).

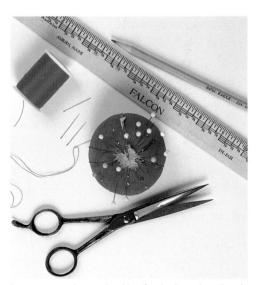

Anyone can make a quilt with a few basic tools and notions.

Beginners' Favorite

THIS IS THE ALL-PURPOSE QUILT—our favorite for beginners—and what could be easier? Squares (or rectangles) separated by a contrasting sashing, afford a blank palette for quilting, appliqué, embroidery, stencils, fabric paint—whatever you and your group choose. Or, you can let the fabric itself steal the show; just use a variety of interesting fabrics with a coordinating sashing to unite them. We have even used this pattern when working with very young children, making the squares of felt and letting each child decorate his own square by gluing cutout felt shapes to the squares.

We offer two variations of this pattern. The first, which we call Bottom-Line Easiest of All, has only nine blocks, a single border, and a small amount of quilting. It could be a nice baby quilt, as in our example, or, with more sophisticated fabrics and different quilting, it could be a charming wall hanging.

The second variation is still simple to construct. (The embellishments, however, are more complicated.) The Alphabet Baby Quilt requires 30 blocks, 26 for the letters and 4 for the corners. We chose reproduction feed sack material with its nostalgic tiny prints and soft colors. (The same quilt done in bold primary colors would be a vibrant adaptation.) We appliquéd the letters (patterns cut freehand from freezer paper) onto the background squares, further securing them with decorative blanket stitching. The embroidered motifs representing each letter are an eye-catching but optional extra. You'll find other examples of one-patch quilts in our Gallery of Quilts on pages 20, 21, 22, 25, and 27.

Bottom-Line Easiest of All

Finished Sizes

Block size: 10 inches (25 cm)
Border width: 4 inches (10 cm)
Quilt size: 38 x 38 inches (.95 x .95m)

Fabric

Blocks and surrounding strips: ¼ yard (22.5 cm) each of nine different fabrics
Border: ⅔ yard (61 cm)
Backing: 1¼ yards (1.15 m)
Bias tape for binding: 5 yards (4.5 m)

Cutting Directions

From each ¼ yard (22.5 cm) of the nine different colors cut the following:
- 8½-inch (21.3 cm) squares, one from each color
- 18 strips, two from each of the colors, each measuring 1½ x 8½ inches (3.8 x 21.3 cm)
- 18 strips, two from each color, each measuring 1½ x 10½ inches (3.8 x 26.7 cm)

From the border fabric, cut:
- Four strips, two measuring 4½ x 30½ inches (11.3 x 76.5 cm)
- Two measuring 4½ x 38½ inches (11.3 x 98 cm)

Assembly

1. Following figure 1, piece your nine blocks, following the color placement in the photo. Remember to press, not iron, the seams.

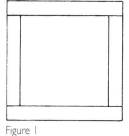

Figure 1

2. Following figure 2, join the blocks in three

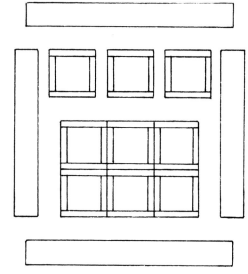

Figure 2

horizontal rows of three blocks each. Press the seams. Now join the three horizontal rows, pinning to match the seams. Press.

3. Following figure 2, add your side borders. Press the seams. Then add the top and bottom borders. Press the seams.
4. Layer the top, batting, and backing. Baste the layers together.
5. Quilt as desired. (We used simple concentric hearts in the squares and straight lines in the narrow strips and in the wide border.)
6. Finish the edge with bias-tape binding. And don't forget your identification panel! (Hanging sleeve is optional.)

Alphabet Baby Quilt

Finished Sizes

Block size: 8 inches (20 cm)
Inner border width: 1 inch (2.5 cm)
Outer border width: 3 inches (7.5 cm)
Quilt: 48 x 56 inches (1.2 x 1.4 m)

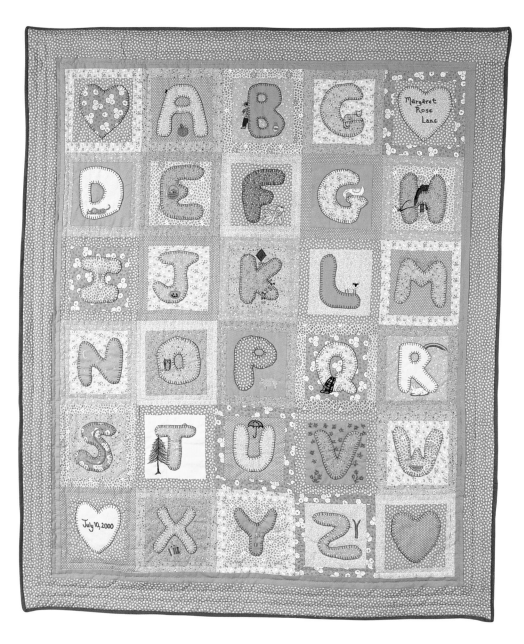

Fabric

Blocks: Fifteen ¼-yard (22.5 cm)
pieces of assorted fabrics*

Inner border: ⅓ yard (30 cm)

Outer border: ⅔ yard (61 cm)

Backing: 3⅓ yards (1.2 m)

Bias binding: 6 yards (5.4 m)

Alphabet Letters: Use leftover fabric

*This will make 30 blocks. You can
cut two blocks and eight edging strips
from each ¼ yard (22.5 cm). This
quilt would also work as a scrap quilt,
with each participant choosing her

own fabric for the blocks and the organizer providing the border fabrics.

Cutting Directions

From the assorted colors, cut:
Thirty 6½-inch (16.3 cm) squares, two from each fabric
Sixty 1½ x 6½-inch (3.8 x 16.3 cm) strips in pairs of assorted colors
Sixty 1½ x 8½-inch (3.8 x 21.3 cm) strips in same pairs of assorted colors

From the inner-border fabric cut:
Six 1½ x 40-inch (3.8 x 101.5 cm) strips. From these strips, piece two 1½ x 42½-inch (3.8 x 108 cm) strips, and two 1½ x 48½-inch (3.8 x 123cm) strips.

From the outer-border fabric cut:
Five 3½ x 40-inch (8.8 x 101.5 cm) strips. From these strips piece two 3½ x 50½-inch (8.8 x 128.5 cm) strips, and two 3½ x 48½-inch (8.8 x 123 cm) strips.

Assembly

1. Following figure 1, piece the 30 blocks.
2. Add appliquéd letters and other desired embellishments before joining the blocks together.
3. Following figure 2, join the blocks in six horizontal rows of five blocks each. Press the seams. Join the horizontal rows, pinning to match the seams. Press.
4. Add the narrow border, sewing on the side borders first. Press the seams.
5. Add the outer border, sewing on the side borders first. Press the seams.
6. Seam the backing together and

press.
7. Layer the top, backing, and batting. Baste the layers together.
8. Quilt as desired. (We outlined the letters and put straight lines in the borders.)
9. Finish the edge with bias-tape binding. Add the identification panel and sleeve (optional).

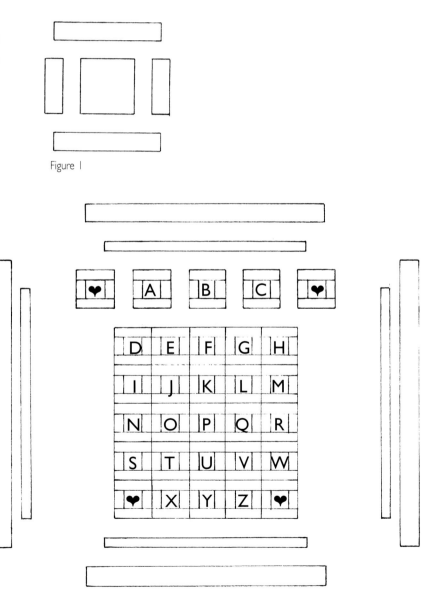

Figure 1

Figure 2

Easy Nine-Patch Single Irish Chain

ALTERNATE A BASIC NINE-PATCH block composed of darks and lights with solid squares of dark or light, and you have achieved a Single Irish Chain. You can make this simple quilt with print fabrics and minimal quilting, or you can use solids, which afford ample space for elaborate quilting—whatever suits your fancy. This pattern is for a crib quilt, but you could easily expand it to make a bed-size quilt. On pages 74 and 91, you'll find two different takes on the Nine-Patch. One uses a carefully chosen variety of fabrics; the other takes a more random approach.

Finished Sizes
Block A (Nine-Patch): 6 inches
(15 cm)
Block B (solid): 6 inches (15 cm)
Border width: 3½ inches (8.8 cm)
Quilt: 37 x 49 inches (.91x 1.25m)

Fabric
Note: The figures given are for rotary cutting or for careful measuring and marking. If you use templates to cut your small squares, you will probably need a little extra fabric.

Block A: ½ yard (45 cm) dark fabric
(¾ yard [68.6 cm] if using templates)
Block A: ½ yard (45 cm) light fabric
(¾ yard [68.6 cm] if using templates)
Block B: ⅔ yard (61cm) dark fabric
Border: ⅔ yard (61cm) dark fabric
Backing: 2 yards (1.8 m)
Bias Binding: 5 yards (4.5 m)

Cutting Directions
FOR BLOCK A:

From the dark fabric, you will need 72 squares, each measuring 2½ x 2½ inches (6.25 x 6.25 cm). To get them, cut five 2½ x 40-inch (6.25 x 101.5 cm) strips. Each strip will yield 16 squares measuring 2½ inches (6.25 cm).

From the light fabric you will need 90 squares, each measuring 2½ x 2½ inches (6.25 x 6.25 cm). Cut six 2½ x 40-inch (6.25 x 101.5 cm) strips.

Each strip will yield 16 squares measuring 2½ inches (6.25 cm).

FOR BLOCK B:

From the dark fabric, you will need 17 squares, each measuring 6½ x 6½ inches (16.3 x 16.3 cm). To get them, cut three 6½ x 40-inch (16.3 x 101.5 cm) strips. Each strip will yield six squares measuring 6½ inches (16.3 cm).

For the borders:
From the dark fabric, cut five 4 x 40-inch (10 x 101.5 cm) strips. From these five strips, construct two 4 x 37½-inch (10 x 95.5 cm) strips by trimming two of the five strips cut above. Then construct two 4 x 42½-inch (10 x 108 cm) strips by adding the necessary lengths.

Assembly

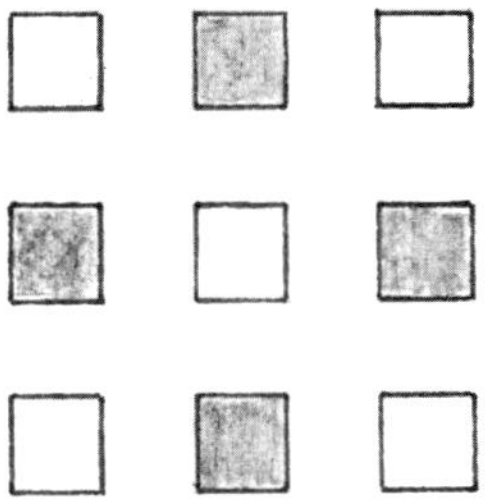

1. Following figure 1, piece 18 Nine-Patch blocks. Press the seams toward the dark fabric.

2. Following figure 2, join the blocks in seven horizontal rows of five blocks each. Press the seams. Now join the horizontal rows, pinning them to match seams. Press seams.

3. Add the border strips, sewing the side strips on first. Press the seams toward border.

4. Seam the backing together and press.

5. Layer the quilt top, batting, and backing. Baste the layers together.

6. Quilt as desired. (For our example, we made a template of a free-form star to quilt in the solid blocks. We quilted diagonal lines through the light squares of the Nine-Patch blocks, extending these lines into the border.)

7. Finish the edge with bias-tape binding. Add the identification panel and hanging sleeve (optional).

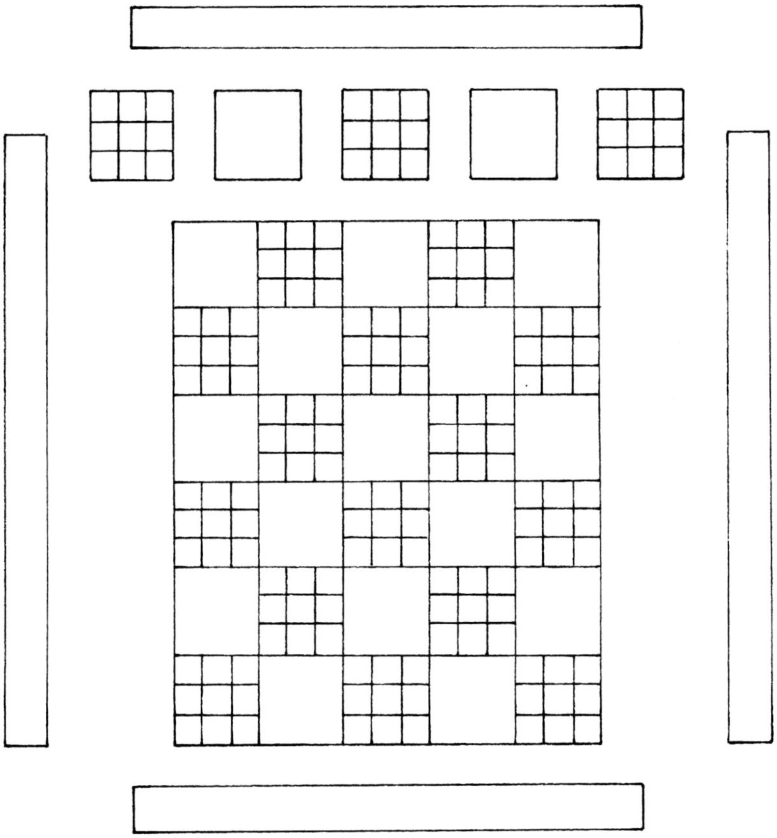

Figure 1

Figure 2

Starry Night
Ninety-nine Block Version

THIS PATTERN LOOKS COMPLEX, but actually is composed of two very easy blocks—the Pinwheel and Shoofly. Our example as shown uses 99 blocks (36 Shoofly and 63 Pinwheel blocks).

This may seem like quite a lot unless you have a large and enthusiastic group with people willing to piece multiple blocks. We chose to use Pinwheels in various shades of blues and purples (and a few deep reds) to lend motion and vibrancy to the background surrounding the yellow Shoofly blocks.

Alternatively, you could make the quilt much easier by substituting solid blocks for some or even all of the Pinwheels, and by using a solid border as directed in the 31-block variation of this pattern. You would still have a beautiful quilt with room for fancy quilting on the blank blocks and borders. We'll give yardage for both options.

Finished Sizes

Shoofly and Pinwheel blocks: 8 inches (20 cm)
Narrow border: 2 inches (5 cm)
Outer Border: 8 inches (20 cm)
Quilt size: 76 x 92 inches (1.9 x 2.2 m)

Fabric

Yellow(s) for Shoofly blocks and narrow border: 1¾ yards (1.6 m)*
Medium-dark blue(s) for Pinwheel and Shoofly blocks, and eight small rectangles in the border: 4½ yards (4.1 m)
Medium-light blue for Pinwheel blocks: 2¼ yards (2 m)**
Deep red for eight Pinwheel blocks: ½ yard (45 cm)
Backing: 9 yards (8.1 m)***
Bias-tape binding: 10 yards (9 m)

*Our yellow yardage was unequally divided among four very similar yellows.
**Again, as with the yellow yardage, we used similar shades of blue in unequal amounts.
***This may seem very generous if you are following the guidelines in step 5 on page 94, but if you try to get by with only 6 yards (5.4 m), you will be awfully close to coming up short.

Cutting Directions

Note: If you are using various shades of one color, you will divide your cutting among them

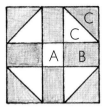

Shoofly Blocks

The following will make 36 Shoofly blocks, 31 for the body of the quilt, and five for the border:

From the yellow(s), cut three strips, each measuring 2½ x 40 inches (6.25 x 101.5 cm). Each strip will yield 16 squares measuring 2½ inches (6.25 cm). You will need a total of 36 squares. This is pattern piece A.

From the medium-dark blue(s), cut nine strips, each measuring 3½ x 40 inches (8.8 x 101.5 cm). Each strip will yield 16 rectangles measuring 2½ x 3½ inches (6.25 x 8.8 cm). You will need a total of 144 rectangles. This is pattern piece B.

From the medium-dark blue(s), cut eight strips, each measuring 3⅞ x 40 inches (9.6 x 101.5 cm). Each strip will yield 10 squares measuring 3⅞ inches (9.6 cm). You will need a total of 72 squares. Following figure 1, cut the squares on the diagonal to yield 144 triangles. This is pattern piece C.

Figure 1

From the yellow(s), cut eight strips, each measuring 3⅞ x 40 inches (9.6 x 101.5 cm). Each strip will yield 10 squares measuring 3⅞ inches (9.6 cm). You will need a total of 72 squares. Following figure 1, cut the squares on the diagonal to yield 144 triangles. This is pattern piece C also.

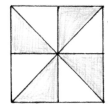

Pinwheel Blocks

The following will make 63 Pinwheel blocks: 32 for the body of the quilt and 31 for the border:

From the medium-dark blue(s), cut 16 strips, each measuring 4⅞ x 40 inches (12 x 101.5 cm). Each strip will yield eight squares measuring 4⅞ inches (12 cm). You will need a total of 126 squares. Cut each square on the diagonal to yield 252 triangles.

From the medium-light blue(s), cut 14 strips, each measuring 4⅞ x 40 inches (12 x 101.5 cm). Each strip will yield eight squares measuring 4⅞ inches (12 cm). You will need a total of 110 squares. Cut each square on the diagonal to yield 220 triangles.

From the red fabric, cut two strips, each measuring 4⅞ x 40 inches (12 x 101.5 cm). Each strip will yield eight squares measuring 4⅞ inches (12 cm). You will need 16 squares. Cut each square on the diagonal to yield 32 triangles.

For the medium-dark blue rectangles near the corners of the border, cut two strips, each measuring 2½ x 40 inches (6.25 x 101.5 cm). Each strip will yield four rectangles measuring 2½ x 8½ inches (6.25 x 21.3 cm). You will need eight rectangles.

For the narrow yellow border, cut seven strips, each measuring 2½ x 40 inches (6.25 x 101.5 cm). You will need to piece the strips to attain the proper lengths for the sides and the top and bottom. For the sides, you will need two pieced

strips, each with a length of 72½ inches (1.85 m). For the top and bottom you will need two pieced strips, each with a length of 60½ inches (1.51 m).

Assembly

Note: See pages 133 and 134 for more detailed instructions.

1. Following figure 2, piece the 36 Shoofly blocks together.

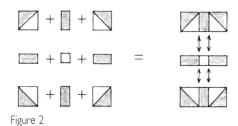

Figure 2

2. Following figure 3, piece the 63 Pinwheel blocks together.

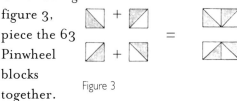

Figure 3

3. Following figure 4, join the blocks in nine horizontal rows of seven blocks each. Press the seams. Now join the horizontal rows, pinning to match the seams. Press.

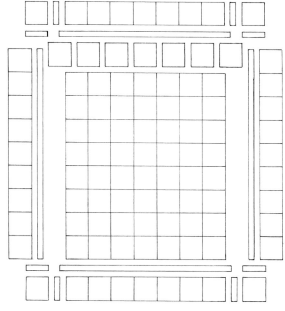

Figure 4

4. Add the narrow yellow borders, sewing on the side borders first, then the top and bottom borders. Press the seams away from the yellow.

5. Referring to figure 4, piece the outer side borders. Note that the side strips begin and end with blue rectangles. Press the seams. Next, sew the side borders to the quilt. Try to eyeball the blocks to get the horizontal seams to match up, even though they are separated by the yellow border. Press the seams.

6. Referring to figure 4, piece your top and bottom borders. Note the changed placement of the blue rectangles. Sew the top and bottom borders to the quilt. Again, try to line up the blocks visually. Press the seams.

7. Seam the backing together and press (see step 13 on page 109). Layer the top, batting, and backing. Baste the layers together.

8. Quilt as desired, or follow figure 5 for a suggested quilting pattern.

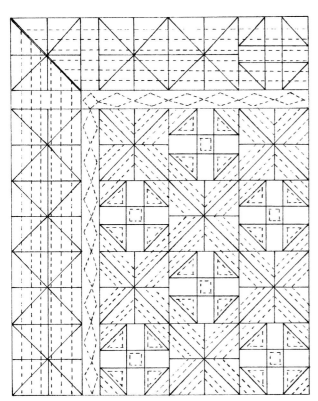

Figure 5

9. Finish the edge with bias-tape binding. Add the identification panel and sleeve (optional).

VARIATION

31-Block Version

Fabric

Yellow for the Shoofly blocks and narrow border: 1½ yards (1.4 m)
Blue for the Shoofly blocks: 1¾ yards (1.6 m)
Blue for the solid blocks: 2 yards (1.8 m)
Blue for the border: 2¼ yards (2 m)
Backing: 9 yards (8.1 m)
Bias binding: 10 yards (9 m)

Cutting Directions

The following will make 31 Shoofly blocks:

From the yellow, cut two strips, each measuring 2½ x 40 inches (6.25 x 101.5 cm) . Each strip will yield 16 squares measuring 2½ inches (6.25 cm). You will need 31 squares. This is pattern piece A.

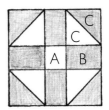

From the blue, cut eight strips, each measuring 3½ x 40 inches (8.8 x 101.5 cm). Each strip will yield 16 rectangles measuring 2¼ x 3½ inches (6.25 x 8.8 cm). You will need 124 rectangles. This is pattern piece B.

From the blue, cut seven strips, each measuring 3⅞ x 40 inches (9.6 x 101.5 cm). Each strip will yield 10 squares measuring 3⅞ inches (9.6 cm). You will need 62 squares. Cut each square on the diagonal to yield 124 triangles. This is pattern piece C.

From the yellow, cut seven strips, each measuring 3⅞ by 40 inches (9.6 x 101.5 cm). Each strip will yield 10 squares measuring 3⅞ inches (9.6 cm). You will need 62 squares. Cut each square on the diagonal to yield 124 triangles. This is pattern piece C also.

From the blue, cut eight strips, each measuring 8½ x 40 inches (21.3 x 101.5 cm). Each strip will yield four squares measuring 8½ inches (21.3 cm). You will need 32 squares. These will be your solid blocks.

For the narrow yellow border, cut seven strips, each measuring 2½ x 40 inches (6.25 x 101.5 cm). You will need to piece the strips to attain the proper lengths for the sides and the top and bottom. For the sides, you will need two pieced strips, each with a length of 72½ (1.8 m) inches. For the top and bottom, you will need two pieced strips, each with a length of 60½ inches (1.5 m).

For the outer blue border, cut four strips, each measuring 8½ x 76½ inches (21.3 x 191.25 cm). Note that you are cutting your fabric *lengthwise* this time rather than across its width.

Assembly

Note: See page 134 for more detailed instructions.

1. Following figure 1, piece the 31 Shoofly blocks together.

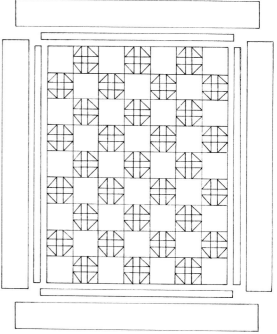

Figure 1

2. Following figure 2, join the Shoofly and solid blocks in nine horizontal rows of seven blocks each. Press the seams. Now join the horizontal rows, pinning to match the seams. Press.

Figure 2

3. Add the narrow yellow borders, sewing on the side borders first, then the top and bottom. Press the seams away from yellow.

4. Add the wide, blue outer borders, sewing on the side borders first, then the top and bottom borders. Press the seams.

5. Seam the backing together and press. Layer the top, batting, and backing. Baste the layers together. Quilt as desired.

6. Finish the edge with bias-tape binding. Add the identification panel and sleeve (optional).

Sample: Organizer's Instructions to the Participants

NOTE TO THE ORGANIZER: Following are the step-by-step instructions for Pattern III, Starry Night, the ninety-nine block version, which we enclosed in the kit to the participants. Though these are specific to a particular quilt, the format illustrates how to organize the information and the amount of detail you will need to provide to the participants. Use these as a guideline for writing your own instructions, modifying them to suit your project.

As the organizer, be aware of the number of kits you will need to send out. For this particular quilt we needed to make up 99 kits, one for each block. We made 63 Pinwheel kits and 36 Shoofly kits. The Pinwheel kits consisted of eight kits, each with four red triangles and four blue triangles, and 55 kits, each kit containing four medium-dark and four medium-light triangles. The Shoofly kits consisted of 36 kits, each containing one yellow pattern piece A, four blue pattern piece B rectangles, four yellow pattern piece C triangles, and four blue pattern piece C triangles.

When writing your instructions, keep a few general principles in mind. Always include a direction to read the directions! You cannot remind participants about the ¼-inch (.5 cm) seam allowance enough. In the instructions you will see illustrations. You will need to provide thumbnail sketches of the blocks in various stages of assembly to give your participants a visual aid. Even experienced quilters appreciate

these, and they will save you from receiving squares that are assembled incorrectly. Include a list of what the kit contains (see step 2 below).

Sample Instructions for Pinwheel Kit

Important: Read directions thoroughly before beginning. It's very important that you use an accurate ¼-inch (.5 cm) seam allowance. The finished quilt contains many small seams, and if they are "off" a little, the finished quilt will be "off" a lot.

1. This is what your finished block will look like.
Be sure to place your darks and lights as they appear in the drawing.

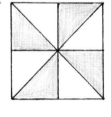

2. This kit contains eight triangles of equal size, four dark and four light. (Red, if you have it, is considered a light.)

3. Press all the pieces, then lay them out as in the illustration of the block in step 1.

4. Match up each light triangle with a dark triangle, right sides together (facing). Sew each pair together along the long, diagonal edge. (This is a bias edge and will stretch if you pull on it, so try not to!)

5. Carefully press the sewn-together triangles open to form a square, making sure to press the seam toward the darker fabric. Be careful not to stretch the square as you press! After pressing, you will have four squares.

6. Measure each square. It should be 4½ x 4½ inches (11.3 x 11.3 cm). If the square is more than ⅛ inch (.3 cm) off, please carefully pick out your sewing and redo.

7. Assemble your Pinwheel as shown.

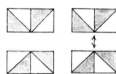 **Note**: Press and measure for accuracy at each step. If your finished block measures ¼ inch (.5 cm) under or over the desired 8½ inches (21.3 cm), that's allowable.

Sample Instructions for the Shoofly Kit

Important: Read directions thoroughly before beginning. It's very important that you use an accurate ¼-inch (.5 cm) seam allowance. The finished quilt contains many small seams, and if they are "off" a little, the finished quilt will be "off" a lot.

1. This is what your finished block will look like:

2. This kit contains one small yellow square, four blue rectangles, four yellow triangles, four blue triangles.

3. Press all the pieces, then lay them out as in the illustration of the block in step 1.

4. Match up each yellow triangle to one blue triangle, right sides together (facing). Sew each pair together along the long diagonal edge. (This is a bias edge and will stretch if you pull on it, so try not to!)

5. Carefully press the sewn-together triangles open to form a square, making sure to press the seam toward the darker fabric. Be careful not to stretch the square as you press! After pressing, you will have four blue and yellow squares.

6. Measure each square. It should be 3½ x 3½ inches (8.8 x 8.8 cm). If the square is more than ⅛ inch (.3 cm) off, please carefully pick out your sewing and redo.

7. Assemble your Shoofly as shown.

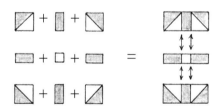

Note: Press and measure for accuracy at each step. If your finished block measures ¼ inch (.5 cm) over or under the desired 8½ inches (21.3 cm), that's allowable.

Quilting Terms

Appliqué The attaching of a small piece of fabric to a larger background piece of fabric by hand or machine stitching.

Art quilt A quilt made for display, not use. Often nontraditional in appearance.

Backing Fabric used for the bottom layer of a quilt.

Backstitch In hand sewing, to loop back over the stitch you've just taken for additional strength.

Baste To join together temporarily the three layers of a quilt with long, hand stitches.

Batting The fluffy filler that is the middle layer of a quilt.

Bias The stretchy diagonal grain of a fabric. Opposite of straight grain.

Bias Tape or Binding Strips of fabric cut on the bias, used as edging for a quilt.

Blind stitch An almost invisible hand-sewing stitch used to sew down edges.

Block The design unit of many quilts. Sometimes called a square, whether square-shaped or otherwise.

Community Quilt A quilt made by many hands. Also called a Group Quilt.

Ease-In To adjust the lengths (by pinching or pulling) of two slightly unequal fabric edges in order to sew them together.

I.D. Panel A small label, permanently affixed to the back of a quilt, containing pertinent information about the quilt.

In-the-Ditch Quilting done as close as possible to a seamline or appliqué edge.

Organizer The person (or persons) who plans and oversees the making of a group quilt.

Outline Quilting Quilting done ¼ inch (.5 cm) away from seams or appliqué pieces.

Pieced Square A block made up of various fabric pieces sewn together according to a pattern.

Quilt Originally a bed cover made of two layers of fabric with a fluffy filling in the middle, the layers being joined together by stitching through all three layers. Now, quilts are not necessarily bedcovers, but can be employed decoratively. (See Art Quilt.)

Quilt-As-You-Go Method of quilting individual blocks, each with its own batting and backing, before assembling them into a quilt.

Quilter's Choice A block in which a quilter is given a piece of background fabric, a theme, maybe a color range, or some other guideline, and asked to make her own decisions as to what will go on the block.

Quilting Small, even running stitches through all three layers of a quilt. Often in decorative patterns.

Rotary Cutting A fabric cutting system that uses a handheld cutter with a sharp rotary blade, a mat (sometimes printed with a grid), and a clear plastic ruler (usually with measuring lines or grids). Very efficient, once you get the hang of it.

Sashing Fabric strips that separate blocks in a quilt top.

Scrap Quilt A quilt made up of fabric on hand, usually many different prints and colors, often chosen somewhat at random.

Seam Allowance The tiny, usually ¼-inch (.5 cm) area of fabric between the sewn seam and the raw edge of the fabric.

Sleeve A strip of fabric sewn to the back of a quilt through which a rod can be inserted to facilitate hanging for display.

Square See Block.

Straight Grain The top to bottom and side to side direction of the threads in a length of fabric.

Template A pattern, usually made from plastic or thin cardboard, which is traced around to mark pattern shapes on fabric for cutting.

Top The uppermost layer of a quilt.

Yard Conversion

⅛ YARD	= 4½ INCHES	(11.3 cm)
¼ YARD	= 9 INCHES	(22.5 cm)
⅓ YARD	= 12 INCHES	(30 cm)
½ YARD	= 18 INCHES	(45 cm)
¾ YARD	= 27 INCHES	(68.5 cm)
1 YARD	= 36 INCHES	(.9 m)

Bibliography

BASICS

Fons, Marianne, and Liz Porter. *American Country Scrap Quilts.* Emmaus, PA. Rodale Press, Inc., 1995.

Fons, Marianne, and Liz Porter. *Quilter's Complete Guide.* Birmingham, AL. Oxmoor House, 1993.

Learn How Book. Coates and Clark Book 170-C. New York, NY. Coats and Clark, Inc., 1975.

Reader's Digest. *Complete Guide to Needlework.* Pleasantville, NY/ Montreal. The Reader's Digest Association, Inc., 1979.

Snook, Barbara. *Needlework Stitches.* New York. Crown Publishers, Inc., 1963.

Townswick, Jane. Edited by Suzanne Nelson. *Quiltmaking Tips and Techniques.* Emmaus, PA. Rodale Press, Inc., 1994.

HISTORY AND INSPIRATION

America's Quilts. Created by the Country's Best Quilters. New York, NY. Gallery Books/ W.H. Smith Publishers, Inc., 1990.

Jenkins, Susan, and Linda Seward. *The American Quilt Story, the How-to and Heritage of a Craft Tradition.* Emmaus, PA. Rodale Press., 1991.

Pottinger, David. *Quilts From The Indiana Amish, A Regional Collection.* New York, NY. E.P. Dutton, 1983.

Regan, Jennifer. *American Quilts, A Sampler of Quilts and their Stories.* New York, NY. Gallery Books/W.H. Smith Publishers, Inc., 1989.

Wahlman, Maude Southwell. *Signs and Symbols, African Images in African-American Quilts.* New York, NY. Studio Books/Penguin Books, Inc., 1993.

PATTERNS

Beyer, Jinny. *Patchwork Patterns.* McLean, VA. EPM Publications, Inc., 1979.

Beyer, Jinny. *The Quilter's Album of Blocks and Borders.* McLean, VA. EPM Publications, Inc., 1980.

Macho, Linda. *Quilting Patterns.* New York, NY. Dover Publications, Inc., 1984.

Pellman, Rachel T. *Amish Quilt Patterns.* Intercourse, PA. Good Books, 1984.

PERIODICALS

Quilter's Newsletter Magazine. Box 59019, Boulder, CO 80323-9019. USA and Canadian 1-800-477-6089.
http://www.quiltersnewsletter.com

Acknowledgments

We are grateful to our publisher, Rob Pulleyn, for advice, suggestions, and encouragement. To Jane LaFerla, our editor, who guided us with a light touch. To Justin Skemp, who helped his mother make the transition from manual typewriter to computer, facilitating the production of our manuscript. To Libby Woodruff, who spent a day with us, looking over the manuscript for errors and omissions. To Jim Woodruff, the designer of our quilting frame, for supplying us with a drawing of it. And to all the quilters whose work and words are the heart of this book.

Index